WHAT IS THIS THING CALLED LOVE?

The Essential Book For The Single Woman

William Glasser, M.D. and Carleen Glasser

Books by Dr. Glasser that relate to this book
All published by HarperCollins:

The Quality School
Choice Theory
The Language of Choice Theory
Reality Therapy In Action

All of these books are available at bookstores and from
the William Glasser Institute.

"This book helped me to understand that I don't have to go to bed with a man to keep his interest. For too many men, sex has nothing to do with love."
- Diane S.

"I used to let men control me and I thought I could control them. This book got me in control of my own life, the only life I can or even want to control."
- Linda W.

"I want to get married. This book explains that marriage is not an old fashioned idea. It's as valid today as it ever was."
- Sara P.

"I threw four years of my life away on a man who kept telling me he loves me. This book told me what went wrong and how to keep it from ever happening again."
- Julie K.

"Finding out about the seven deadly habits was worth a hundred times the price of this book. Now I know what not to do and what to watch out for in my next relationship."
- Barbara M.

"The last chapter in this book is brilliant. It's an original way of thinking about love that helped me realize what I'm looking for in a relationship."
- Lynn F.

"I'm going to give one of these books to everyone of my single friends. It's filled with useful ideas."
- Maureen D.

"After reading this book I got a clear picture of the specific qualities I'm looking for in the man for me. That's why after all these years I think I've found the right one."

- Jane A.

"I finally broke up with a man who said he loved me. This book explained why I left him. He was in love but not with me."

- Brenda U.

"Reading this book made me realize that until I love and respect myself, I'll have a hard time loving anyone else."

- Debbie C.

"The story of my life was revealed on the pages of this book. I wish I'd had it sooner."

- Kathy H.

For Susan

Author's Note

Before this book was printed, we tested the manuscript on a few single women we know. They were very enthusiastic and told us how much it would have helped them if they'd had this information before now. We were encouraged but we'd like to get more feedback from women we don't know.

If this book has helped you to move out of a going nowhere, living together relationship and to start using the new definition of love we offer here, will you please write us and tell us about your experience. Nothing helps people more than understanding the experiences of others like themselves.

Please feel free to write in some detail, we're patient readers, too much is better than too little. And give us your permission to edit it and then use it in a later edition. We would not publish anything without first getting your permission. Your identity would, of course, be kept completely confidential.

Please address your remarks and any questions to us at our office.

Bill and Carleen Glasser
22024 Lassen St., Suite 118, Chatsworth, CA 91311
Fax: 818-700-0555; Phone: 818-700-8000
E-Mail wginst@earthlink.net

One

"Ann, I love you very much. You know how much you mean to me. But please, I'm not quite ready yet."

After a year of begging that's getting me more and more down, he's still telling me how much he loves me. But now he's added,

"Don't pressure me."

"Finally...... I stopped begging and came right out with,

"Mark, I'm not pressuring you. We've been together three years, If you don't want to marry me, say so and I'll never ask you again."

But he just keeps repeating,

"I love you, Ann. You're an amazing woman. I don't know what I'd do without you. You know I want to marry you."

But, not one word about when.... After that I made up my mind to keep my mouth shut and marriage became the unspoken "M" word in our lives..... My friends keep telling me,

"Be patient. Don't you know how lucky you are to have such a good looking, successful guy who adores you? Be cool. Give him time.... If you keep bugging him he'll never ask you."

But my gentle loving mother gave me a jolt. I can still hear her saying,

"Wake up, Ann. He's never going to make up his mind. You're twenty-seven years old. You're throwing your life away for something that's not going to happen. Telling you he loves you is the only thing he's better at now than he was last year."

My mother had never come on that strong before.... I started to cry.

"But Mom, I love him. Just the idea of life without Mark...."

My mother held me as I sobbed. But this time she didn't give in to my tears.

"Ann, tell me..... Do you have any idea what love really is? You keep saying, I love him, but what does it mean? What does he mean when he says it to you? Ann, here you are sobbing in my arms talking about love. If that's love, I feel sorry for you."

Blowing my nose and wiping my eyes, I moaned.

"I don't know what love is. Nobody knows what love is. I only know that Mark's been my whole life for three years. The idea of giving him up, I can't deal with it."

But that night when I went home to our empty apartment, more and more he's gone on business, I got to thinking about what my mother asked me. What's love? What is it? And if I'm so miserable, why is Mark my whole life? All my girl friends are just like me, we keep talking about love but who's happy? For God's sake, shouldn't love be happy? Am I crazy to be so desperate to get married? My mother was right. What's love anyway? Why doesn't it mean the same to Mark as it does to me?"

*****

At the end of a lecture to a group of schoolteachers about relating better to kids, I touched briefly on love in adult relationships. Ann was there. After the lecture, she stayed and asked if we could talk. I wasn't in a hurry; we started to chat. After a few minutes she introduced herself and then began to come to the point.

"I know you work a lot with school problems but you're a psychiatrist, aren't you?"

I nodded.

"Don't you see a lot of women who are having trouble with love? I know a lot of women who go to therapists."

"You're right, I do see a lot of women, I see men, too, but more women."

"I'm sorry if I'm being nosy but when you see them, what's wrong? Why do so many women go to therapists?"

"Love problems, marriage problems, living together problems, it's not easy to be a woman today."

"I know this may sound like a weird question but have you ever tried to help them figure out what love is? I mean they're all upset about it but do they actually know what it is."

"I'm not sure I understand what you're driving at."

"Okay, I teach algebra. None of my students have any idea what math is much less algebra. How can you expect a kid to be able to solve math problems if they don't even know what it is? I know it may sound far-fetched but I think most of the people you see who are upset about love don't even know what it is. I know I don't."

I thought for a moment and then said,

"I do help people with love but I've never really tried to help them figure out what it is. I guess I've taken it for granted that they know what it is..... You know, if I had to come up with a good answer to your question right now, I don't think I could."

"Don't you think a psychiatrist who deals all day with love problems should be able to answer that question? Is it so much harder to define than algebra that it can't be answered?"

"I think it's a lot more complicated than algebra but, you're right, it should have a definition...... I guess you have a personal interest in finding out what it is?"

"I have a very strong personal interest in finding out what it is. I think I'm in love and the guy keeps telling me he loves me. But I don't think either of us has any idea what we're talking about. I keep saying to myself, `How am I going to find love, if I don't know what it is' And I really don't. Actually, it's just the opposite. I've been living with a man for three years and I'm more confused about love than I've ever been. He doesn't want to marry me but he keeps telling me he loves me. What in the world does he mean? You're a psychiatrist, don't you think a woman should know what a man means when he says, I love you?"

"Ann, to tell you the truth, I don't know that much about what anyone means when they say, I love you. I doubt if it means the same thing for you as it does for him. I can see your point. We all assume we know what love is but I guess we really don't....... But you're after something, Ann. Do you want something from me?"

"I want you to help me find out what love is. Teach me and I'll be happy to pay you. I have a little money from my grandmother. I think she'd approve of me spending it on this.

*****

What Is This Thing Called Love? is a record of our conversations as we struggled with that question. While I won't attempt to write every word that passed between us, I'll cover the essence of what we talked about. I appreciate what Ann asked because I'm working on a new theory that attempts to explain all human behavior. Since love may be among the most important and least understood of all the behaviors we choose, trying to answer her question could test my theory. A lot of school teachers are reading my book about the theory, it's called *Choice Theory*[1] so I asked Ann if she'd read it and she said she hadn't. I told her that for a while it would be better if she didn't and that was fine with her. I thought, it makes more sense to test the ideas on someone with no prior knowledge of them. She also insisted,

"I want to make it clear that I don't need therapy and I don't expect miracles. All I want to do is talk with you and share ideas. I liked that stuff you were explaining about relationships, it made sense to me."

"I guess finding love, that's the relationship we all have problems with. So if you want to come to my office and talk about love, I think it could be interesting."

"I'd like to do that but I'm not asking for therapy, I don't think there's anything wrong with me."

"I don't think there's anything wrong with you either, I don't think there's anything wrong with anyone who wants to take a good look at what love is."

"And since it's not therapy, I don't think you should charge me very much."

---

[1]William Glasser (1998), *Choice Theory*, HarperCollins, New York.

"I'm not going to charge you anything."

"Why not? Your time's valuable."

"Because I've never done this before. I charge for therapy, I'm an expert there..... but love, I don't think there are any experts on that subject..... This is like research. If we find something out, it could help a lot of people. Mostly women but men, too, for that matter. They may not come for therapy but I don't think they know anymore about love than women. And if we find anything out it's going to be as much your doing as mine. But the real reason I can't charge you is I'm not sure I'll be able to help you learn anymore than you know now. Like I said, I'm an expert on counseling, I don't see myself as an expert on love."

Two

A week after we met, we got together in my office. There was a lot about her that told me she was used to taking care of herself. Her looks, dress, makeup, hairdo, her whole demeanor suggested competence. She was quite attractive but it was the competence you'd notice more than her looks. As I got to know her, I think it would be fair to say that she was trying to approach understanding love as she would a difficult math problem. It would take effort but it was solvable. Ann did not have a mind that would wander around, she would stay on track. After a short preliminary discussion to hear the basics of her life with Mark, I started in by saying,

"Tell me, Ann, what have you learned about love so far in your life? Any kind of love, not just with Mark, just some general idea where you're coming from."

"I had a caring childhood. Lot's of love from my mother and that's never ended. We have our spat's, I mean we disagree a lot. But never any hard feelings. She and my sister are a lot alike, very strong opinions and not afraid to say what's on their minds. But I can always feel her love so no matter how much we argue, I'm never really upset for very long. But I also had a lot of love from my Grandma, my Mom's mother. Until she died two years ago I may have been even closer to her than to anyone else."

"In what ways?"

"She never told me what to do, never criticized me for what I did. I think she loved me even more than she loved my mother. I felt very secure with all that love. Until Mark, I really never have missed the love of a man because I never had any. My father left when I was fourteen and that was the last I saw of him. My mother says he loved me but, if he did, I don't remember it. I mean he didn't abuse me, it was more like he ignored me. He was so involved with himself, he didn't even know I was there.

"How about sexual love? What about that part of your life?"

"I didn't know anything when I was little, like about sex between my mother and father, but I was aware they never got along. I guess the first time I thought seriously about sex was when my sister started doing it. Edith's two years older and she started having sex when she was fourteen. She'd tell me about it but it didn't seem that great to me. As far as I was concerned, the guy was a jerk. Whatever love was, it didn't seem she had much of it with David. I couldn't see what she saw in him but she got pregnant and they got married when she was only sixteen. She was a perfect negative role model. If she did it, I didn't want to do it. Edith's twenty-nine now and she has a thirteen year old daughter she's raising by herself. Well, not totally by herself, my mother and I, we help her all we can. The marriage to David, if you can call it a marriage, lasted three years. He was a druggie and a pusher; he's now doing time in jail. But a few years later she married again and now she's divorced from that guy too. She always seems to have a guy but as far as love, I don't think she's ever really had it with a man. I think she's been closer to Mark than to any guy she's ever had. Lately, though, even Edith's been saying I ought to put pressure on him, that I'm crazy to let him get away with all I've given him and not marry me. She's even suggested I get pregnant, that would make him marry me..... A lot of good it did her."

"What was wrong with the second guy, was he a bum too?"

"No, not at all. He was very responsible where work was concerned and she was able to stay home with her daughter, Margo, for a few years. But right from the start Margo hated him and he hated her, that part was a disaster. The way I saw it he never really loved my sister. All he wanted her for was sex. When she got pregnant he was furious, he made her have an abortion. He said he didn't want kids, ever, and the marriage fell apart. As soon as they divorced, she moved back home. Mom's always helped her with Margo. She doesn't talk about it anymore but I think she still spends an occasional weekend with her ex. But when she did talk about it, there wasn't much love in those get-togethers that I could see."

"How about you?"

"Getting involved with boys in high school was not for me. I dated but no sex. What I did was pay attention in class. Unlike most of the kids I grew up with, I liked school. I was a virgin when I went off to college but in my sophomore year I got involved. It was with a married man, actually one of my math professors. He was gentle and loving and kept telling me how much he cared about me but he never used the word love and never intimated he loved me. He did get a big kick out of being my first lover, I guess he was the first for a lot of girl's in his classes. I was pretty sure I wasn't the only one while he was seeing me but that didn't bother me. I had no illusions where he was concerned. It was loving, but not really love. All the time, he kept encouraging me to date guys my own age. While I was with him, I dated but I didn't get involved with anyone until the beginning of my senior year. That's when I met a Pakistani graduate student in physics. We had a lot to talk about and we actually lived together for the last six months before I graduated. When I moved here to teach, he had at least two more years on his doctorate and we said goodbye. I was upset about it for a while but from the beginning I'd never really thought it'd go anywhere."

"Tell me about Mark,"

"When I came back here to teach, I dated a little but no one seriously. My job is next to impossible. I put a lot of effort into trying to get my students to even admit the existence of math and when a few do, I think I've really accomplished something. I don't like to drink so I began to hang out at a local Starbucks, it kinda became my home away from home. That's where I met Mark and in no time we were in love. I'd never felt like that before, it was wonderful. We didn't always get along great, but we enjoyed making up after our little quarrels. I liked it that he was intelligent, that he had a good job and he'd never been married. He's great looking and only two years older than me. On paper we looked perfect. I, especially, liked that he didn't come on to me. We dated for four months before we went to bed. We finally decided we'd do it one weekend in a fancy hotel and we stayed in that room making love for thirty-six hours. After that we agreed there was no way we could think of being separated and immediately started looking for an apartment. That's when we had our first big disagreement. I wanted to make a life with him, to move into a really nice place that had a sense of permanence and he was nervous about that. Well, we argued but he finally gave in. We're still there. I keep putting things into it, I have no intention of leaving it no matter what happens with him. I didn't realize it at the time but I guess renting that nice place and fixing it up was a bigger commitment to me than he wanted to make. I was so in love and I trusted him so much, I just took it for granted he felt the same way and that we'd get married. It took him awhile to accept the nice apartment and we were very happy for the whole first year. I was so in love that I didn't even think about marriage. I had my career. I didn't want children right away, there was no hurry. Anyway, we talked and joked a lot about being married and having a family and he kept telling me how much he loved me every time we'd turn around. But after that first year, I really began to think a lot about getting married and started to mention it to Mark. He said, `I love you but we need to wait.' Well, to make a long story short, I didn't say much for another year. But this past year I've begun to harp on it. I've argued, threatened and, even begged but he still says he's not ready. And his traveling has really begun to get on my nerves. I hate how much he has to travel. And all his hesitation about marriage. Maybe if we lived in different times, I might've dropped him by now but I have a problem with starting to date again. I dread it. That's a big part of what's keeping me with Mark. All the attractive men want to go right to bed. The idea of going to bed with a variety of strange men after three years of good love making with Mark is more than I can cope with. I'm twenty-seven. It's only three years but times have changed, it's going to be hard to find the kind of man I want who'll be as patient as Mark. I'm afraid of catching a disease, I really am. The idea of letting a man I hardly know be with me is, I don't know the word. I was going to say repugnant, it's not that bad but it's close. It's just so much easier to stay where I am."

"If he asked you to marry him now, would you accept?"

"Of course, I would. If he asked me, I think he'd mean it. I think we'd have a good chance for a successful marriage. But don't worry, Mark's not about to take that step. Saying, I love you, but be patient, seems to be as far as he's willing to go. Lately, I even think it may be as far as he's able to go. Is there anything else you want to know?"

I said I think that's enough for today and we made an appointment for the following week. I also told her that starting next week, I wanted to tape record our sessions but I would give the tape to her at the end of each session. This way she could listen to it at home if she wanted to go back over what we talked about. She agreed, signed a release, and said,

"I don't know how much telling you all that helped me learn about love but I feel better that you know where I stand. And I think I know where I stand better for telling you. I'm really looking forward to talking with you next week."

Three

All that next week I thought about Ann's story and how typical it was. So many men and women are having difficulty connecting love with marriage. Can love really exist between a man and a woman if she wants to get married and he doesn't? And if it can, what exactly is that love? When Ann arrived she was eager to continue our new venture, I said,

"Let's begin where you began when you were young, with the love you and your mother have for each other.... How does your mother show you she loves you?"

"She seems to know what's in my head. Like I said, we do have our disagreements but in the end she's mostly on my side. She may point out some facts on the other side but that's to help me, never to put me down. And she's always loving. Her voice is filled with care when we talk and her face lights up whenever she sees me. Until this year, we never had a serious argument."

"This year?"

"It's what's going on now with Mark. A few weeks ago she said I should break up with him. That I was wasting time hanging on. But then when I didn't listen to her and just kept hanging on with him, she began to agree with what Edith's been telling me, push him harder to marry me. And this happened just when I've begun to think that I'm making a mistake by not dropping him. If I tell her that's what I'm thinking about, it'll drive her nuts. So for the first time since I was a teenager, I've been reluctant to talk to her because no matter what I say, I know it's going upset her."

"Have you told her to back off, to let you work it out on your own?"

"I've tried but she doesn't listen. Like I said, it's gotten to the point where I don't talk about Mark anymore. Where I used to get a lecture on how bad he is for me, now I get a lecture on how good he is for me. My Mom's as confused as I am. Oh, I still love her, don't get me wrong. But it bothers me that one way or another, she's so set on what I should do with Mark that I can't talk with her."

"I guess you're right. This thing with Mark is driving her nuts. But what would you like her to do when she sees you making what she believes is a big mistake? I guess, either way."

"Talk to me, give me her opinion but don't be so sure she knows what's best for me. In the beginning when I told her to leave it alone she did. But recently she's been relentless."

"But you still love her. What could you do that might allow you to talk with her about Mark again no matter which way she wants you to go?"

"That's a hard one. I don't want to argue with her, it's easier to just drop it."

"Ann, right now you're dealing with both Mark and your mother by trying to sweep the problem under the rug."

"So what? That's what everyone does. Why keep talking about something that gets everyone upset?"

"But shouldn't it be just the opposite? If you really love each other, shouldn't love lead to honest communication?"

"Are you serious? When people who care for each other disagree, honest talk's impossible. I can talk honestly to you because I don't love you. But not to my mother, not to Mark. Not even to my sister. You're a psychiatrist. If everybody in love were honest, you'd be out of business."

"You really don't think love and honesty can co-exist?"

"Not when there's a disagreement. I told you last week, as long as Mark's still trying to make up his mind about marriage, no matter how much he says he loves me, I don't believe him."

"But your mother. You've loved her your whole life. Shouldn't you be able to figure out a way to talk to her about Mark and feel comfortable?"

"You're persistent, aren't you?"

"There must be something you can do. This shutting down about Mark isn't good for your relationship with her, you know that."

I thought to myself, Ann needs the support that comes from having a good relationship with her family, especially, now when she's confused and feeling rejected. Ann said,

"I don't know. No matter what she says I still love her. I don't expect her to be perfect. She wants the best for me even though she's not sure what it is."

I kept looking at her, I didn't want to drop the subject. She said,

"What you say should be possible but I don't know."

She thought for a few minutes and then said,

"I could point out that I'm twenty seven and ask her to stop trying to tell me how to live my life. I mean I could do it in a real loving way and then tell her, `When you do that I can't talk to you about the problem...... And I love you. I want to be able to talk to you about anything.'"

I nodded my appreciation of what she just said and then asked,

"How many times in the past six months has your mother put pressure on you about Mark?"

"In one way or another almost every day. She brings it up whenever we talk or get together."

"So there's no way you couldn't know how she feels?"

"At the time, I always know how she feels but she's worried about me, she can't help it. She keeps badgering me, keeps telling me it's for my own good."

"Have you ever loved someone who didn't try to control you, who didn't know what was best for you when you were having trouble?"

"Only my grandma. She never told me what to do. That doesn't mean she didn't care, I know she cared. But she just loved me and let me be. I could talk to her about anything. I miss her a lot."

"Was your grandma that way with your mother?"

"No, not at all.... just with me. She didn't like my father. Even before he left, she kept throwing digs at my mother like, `You never should have married the bum.' And when he left, she said, `I told you so.' They were bitter about that for years. Thank goodness they made up before she died."

"What do you think's the point of all the questions I've been asking?"

"You're suggesting that maybe love is figuring out how to care without trying to control....... It sounds marvelous..... But is it possible? It isn't only about marriage. In lots of ways I've been trying to control Mark and he does the same with me. My school's filled with teachers who are unhappy with the way their partners treat them. It's all about control. They complain to anyone who'll listen. God knows what they say to each other at home. Or maybe don't say. Like Mark and me, to avoid arguments, we just stop talking about a lot of things. Every woman I know who's with a man is in a battle for control."

"How effective are these battles? Does anyone ever win? I mean have you ever been in a battle that ends with you or Mark saying, `You're right, I was wrong. I appreciate your setting me straight?'"

"Are you kidding? That's never happened with Mark. Or for that matter with the guy I lived with before Mark. People don't give in, it's not the way we are."

"What is the way we are?"

"Whenever we disagree with each other we want our own way. That's why I have so much trouble with my students. I keep forcing them to learn something they see no sense learning. There's no way we can ever be friends. I think some of them actually hate me. But I have to force them, if I didn't, I'd lose my job."

"Do you have to keep forcing Mark? Or your mother?"

"I'm not sure I understand what you mean."

"No one makes you force Mark or your mother, like they make you force your students. When you and Mark have a disagreement, no one is stopping you from saying, `You're right, I didn't think so for a while but now I see what you meant.' He can't always be wrong and you always right."

"But why should I do it? He's never done it with me."

"But we're here to try to understand love. I don't think love can exist very long in a controlling relationship. If Mark were here, I'd ask him the same question."

"Well then maybe he ought to be here."

"Any time he wants to come he's welcome. Talk to him. Ask him to come with you next week. But since you're here and he's not, can you do what we've been talking about?"

"What do you mean, do what?"

"Just for the sake of our research, sometime next week, tell him you agree with him. Don't try to have the last word. Last week, you complained he's out of town a lot. I'm sure you talk about it.

"All the time."

"What does he say when you complain?"

"He says he has to travel if he wants to get ahead in the company. They expect it and they've already told him they have an eye on him for a big promotion. Mark's ambitious and a team player."

"What do you think would happen if you said, `Mark, I've been thinking, we'd be better off if I quit nagging. Your work is important to you, I'm going to stop complaining about your traveling."

"But if I do that, I think he'd travel more. He may be gone for weeks at a time."

"Do you really think your complaining is holding him back now?"

"No, not really.... you're right. If he wants to go, he'll go anyway."

"Mark's traveling is a sore subject between you. See if you can do what I just suggested this coming week as an experiment. I think it might help. You don't have to make a life-long commitment. See what happens for just a week."

"But what if he notices? He'll want to know what I'm doing."

"Tell him the truth. Tell him we're doing some research to try to figure out what love is. Ask him how he feels about it and tell him he's welcome to come in with you next week if he wants to."

"But if he knows it's an experiment, won't that spoil it?"

"I don't think it'll make a bit of difference. It might even work better if he knows you're trying to solve the problem instead of nagging him about it."

"It'll be hard but I'll try...... control's a big issue in love, isn't it?"

"It seems to me it is. I think we'll be talking a lot about control in the coming weeks..... Here's the tape I promised you. If you decide to explain what we're doing to Mark, invite him to listen to it with you. Or by himself, that's up to you. I don't think we've said anything that'd offend him. Tell him he's welcome to come in with you next week if he's in town. Or if he wants to, call me and I'll arrange a time that'll work for him."

Four

Mark was with Ann the next time she came to see me. She introduced him and he seemed glad to be with her. She'd told him it wasn't therapy and explained what we were trying to do. He said he'd listened to the tape twice and thought he understood what I was getting at when we discussed how trying to control each other was hurting their love. Mark signed the release for taping today's discussion and I started by asking him,

"I've been wondering, Mark, did Ann accept that you need to travel and stop complaining about it as I suggested on the tape?"

Ann interrupted. "I did, he was really surprised."

"You'd never done anything like that. That's when I asked you what was going on and you told me about these conversations with Dr. Glasser."

Ann said, "And the tape, we listened to it together, it gave us a lot to think about."

Mark said, "It brought us closer to each other, real close.

Ann added, "We felt like making love, we haven't felt like that in a long time."

"Ann, since we're trying to find out what love is, what do the words *making love* mean to you? And to you too, Mark."

They both looked at me and then at each other. I think they saw the significance of using the word love in a sexual context but they wanted a little more explanation. I continued,

"A lot of people say, *We make love*, but mostly it's a polite euphemism for sex, it may actually have little to do with love. If it means anything more to you than sex, I'd like you to explain what."

Ann said, "It used to mean more to me, a lot more to me. But not nearly as much since we've been going back and forth about marriage."

I said, "Would you agree with that, Mark?"

There was a pause. Ann continued to look at Mark as if she wanted him to say something about why her feeling of love for him had fallen off even though they were still having sex.

"Okay, I feel the same. But that doesn't mean I love you any less. That happens with all couples. In the beginning it's a lot of both, love and sex. But there was a lot more love when we did it after you stopped complaining about my work last week. I felt very loving when you seemed willing to see my point of view."

Ann said, "Okay, but as much as I enjoyed it, I was a little resentful. Am I going to have to give in to everything he wants if we're to have more loving sex? I'm willing to have sex once in a while without much love because I enjoy it, I'm a normal human being. But it's not what I want and I'm worried because that's where we seem to be going."

Mark said, "It's the arguments, the disagreements.... They kill the love part. Sex can put up with bickering, love can't. Like when people have sex after they've had a fight, my brother and his wife do it all the time. That kind of sex is pretty desperate. But if they stop, there'll be nothing left.... There's not much left in that marriage as it is, believe me. The fighting's back in no time and nothing gets solved. I mean they're stuck with each other, they don't want a divorce, it's awful. I keep thinking about their marriage."

"Mark's right. Sex really can't help you get along. You get resentful, you feel as if you're being used. But getting along can sure help your sex life."

"Have you accepted each other's point of view with any other disagreements this past week?"

Mark said, "Since we listened to that tape we haven't had any serious disagreements. Things are definitely better."

I asked cautiously, "I wonder. If things are better, did either of you bring up the subject of marriage?"

"I brought it up but not the way he thought I would. I told him I appreciated last week's closeness but I'm not sure I want to marry him anymore. I mean, for three years he's been telling me he loves me. He knows I want to get married. But the way I feel right now, I don't want to marry a man who doesn't love me enough to want to marry me. This fighting about marriage is killing my love for him. That's the reason I'm here. I call it love, everyone calls it love. But what is it, really? Love doesn't describe how I feel about him right now. Love doesn't describe our relationship at all."

"But that's ridiculous, I love you, I've never said I don't want to marry you."

"Please Mark, I don't want to rehash it, it's enough. And believe me, I didn't come here to try to get you to marry me. I'm here to find out what love is and if I love you enough to want to marry you.... But I'm glad we had a good week and I'm happy you came today. Dr. Glasser, if Mark's willing to give it a try, I'd like him to tell us what he really means when he says, `I love you.'"

"When I say it, I mean it...... But you know how afraid of marriage I am. I told you that from the start. I keep seeing my brother's marriage. He's miserable. And she is, too. I keep thinking, we could end up like that?....... And now you tell me you've got cold feet and that makes me feel awful. I love you, you're my whole life outside of work. That's why I came today. Just that one little suggestion from the doctor and look how well we're getting along."

"One little suggestion that got you what you want and all of a sudden we're getting along so well. And we are, I'll admit it. I don't want to be miserable any more than you do. But that one little suggestion didn't get me what I want. I don't care about your brother's marriage. My sister's miserable too just like your brother. You know the story. Dr. Glasser, she's good looking, she gets offered a lot of sex, mostly from married men, but no love at all that I can see. Compared to me, what she knows about love would fill a thimble. But I'll tell you, Mark, I'm not my sister and you're not your brother. If we have to wait for them to be happy, we'll wait forever...... But what I seem to be finding out so far is what love isn't, like it's not controlling each other. But there must be more to it than that. That's what I'm here to find out."

I said, "I think knowing what it isn't may be as important as knowing what it is. Like when you buy a house. No matter how good it looks, you should find out if it has termites."

"The termites in our relationship are his finding fault with everything. It's not just his not marrying me. It's that he's never really satisfied. It's all his criticizing, it just gets to be a drag."

"Is she right, Mark? Do you spend a lot of time finding fault with the way things are?"

"I do....... But not with her. It's my work. I work for a boss like that idiot in *Dilbert*..... Ann, do I ever criticize you or find fault with you?"

"Not being willing to marry me after all this time, to me that's finding fault with me. You're telling me I'm not worth marrying. As long as I don't bring the subject up, it's not a problem and you're lovey dovey. But I'm not going to spend any more of my life waiting for you to make up your mind. If I can find out some more about love, I'll know more what I'm looking for. Then I think I'll be able to find someone who'll love me enough to marry me."

I said, "I wonder if a person who's quick to criticize and find fault is capable of love?"

Mark blurted out, "She's criticizing me right now with that termite crack. I'm capable of love. Ann, you've been with me for three years, you know I'm capable of love.... Lot's of it."

"Lot's of it would be fine if we could agree on what "it" is. That's why I'm glad you're here. I'll tell you, no matter what love is, this year there's been less of it. Before I marry anyone, I want to be getting more of it not less......... Look at what we're doing right now. We've never had a talk like this. If I hadn't come here, it'd never have crossed your mind to talk with me like this. Doctor, I know this sounds like criticism but I've been worried a lot about how he constantly complains and criticizes. He's right, he doesn't do it much with me but we're not married. Marriage changes things, I'm trying to find out why. Even my sister got along with her second husband before they got married."

"Mark, is there anything you could do to convince her that this decrease in love is just temporary? I think she needs some convincing."

"I don't think our love is decreasing...... Look at last week, how good it was. I love her, what more can I say?"

Ann said, "But that's what I want. I want you to say more. It'll help me make up my mind."

"I hate it when you keep saying that. It's like I'm on probation. If you love me, you should have faith in our future."

"Up to last year I had a lot of faith in our future. I thought you did too. But now I don't think so. You say, if I love you but that's a big *if*. That *if* is why I'm here. So far I've been finding out what love isn't. It's not control, it's not criticism, it's not finding fault or complaining and above all, it's not selfish. And it shouldn't start to fade away after we're together for a few years. It should get stronger and I should feel better about myself and about us, not worse."

"But you complain, a lot, too. All I hear is how tough your job is, the kids won't work, the middle school teachers didn't prepare them to learn. Ann, I'm working my head off so you don't have to work if we have kids.... Don't look at me like that.... I love you and I want to have children with you. That's more than just saying, `I love you.'"

"All of a sudden we're having children?...... How about getting married first?..... You brought that up because you know it's important to me..... That's what you do, Mark, throw up smoke screens when you're uncomfortable.... Doctor, we used to talk a lot about having a family and I enjoyed it. But not anymore."

"Mark, we seem to be getting off the track... Give it a try, tell us what you mean when you say, `I love you?'"

"I want to know what she means when she says she loves me."

"I don't know whether you've noticed but I haven't been saying it lately. I guess you say it so much you didn't realize I've stopped. I'm not going to say it again until I know what it means when I say it. I think we'd be better off if you'd stop, too. I'm doing more than looking for love, I'm trying to find out what I'm looking for."

Mark said, "Okay, so am I. I agree with you on that."

"That's good, that's focused. What love is for each of you is where we ought to be. Unfortunately, our time's almost up.... Here's today's tape, I suggest you both listen to it this coming week...... Mark, do you want to come back next week?"

"Ann, is it okay with you?"

Five

Mark was there with Ann the following week and he immediately told me,

"We had the best week we've had in a long time."

Ann said, "Yeah, we did.... But why? Knowing why is important to me."

Mark interrupted, "Forget about the whys and just enjoy it. Worrying too much why things happen isn't good for us."

"Maybe not for you but it's good for me. We did okay all week because I never once brought up marriage. That's why. What if I'd said, `Okay, you can work all the late hours you want but I want to be married when you do.' Then I'd know you were working for us. Right now I feel you're just working for yourself. But don't worry, that's it, I'm not going to talk about marriage anymore. We're here to talk about love."

I said, "Look, you both agree you had a better week. Let's start from there. Could you tell me, how you actually felt..... I know feelings are hard to describe but if you can come up with some words, I think we could learn something."

Ann said, "How about.... close? I've got to admit I felt closer to him."

"Close is good, anything else?"

Mark said, "See, that's what I was trying to tell you. I felt loved. I haven't felt that much love for a long time."

Ann said, "I did too. But not free. I had to steer clear of the "M" word, you know, kind of watch everything that came out of my mouth. I think people who love each other should be free to say what they feel.... Sure, be polite and not hurt each other..... But maybe even more than that. I think love means that we should encourage each other to say what's on our minds. All we did was declare a temporary truce."

Mark thought for a moment,

"She may not have felt free but I began to trust her. I didn't have to worry about her saying she wasn't sure she wanted to marry me. I can't deal with her saying that."

Ann said, "To you, trust is being sure of me, sure that I won't do or say anything to upset you, sure I want what you want. That's what I did all week long. We felt close because we swept the problems

33

under the rug, that's what we do. We talked about that, Doctor, remember? So you were sure of me but what about me being sure of you, trusting you, doesn't that count for anything?"

Mark said, "We didn't sweep the problems under the rug. Getting married isn't a problem. I've never said we won't get married. It's all the talk about it, arguing about it. We were better off keeping our mouths shut and avoiding the pain. That's what we did all last week and we had a lot of love. What's wrong with that?"

I said, "It won't work. You can't solve problems by avoiding them. If you love each other, you need to find a way to talk about problems that works. Right now, marriage is your big problem. Why can't you talk about it?"

Ann said, "That's what I've been trying to say...."

I interrupted, "Please, maybe this'll help. What else didn't you do all week that you've been doing for years?"

Both Ann and Mark looked at me as if to say, what do you mean?"

"I believe that things you've been saying to each other a lot lately were missing from your conversations last week. Things that would've killed the little truce you had. You got rid of some of them and it felt better."

Mark said, "What was missing were most of the put-downs and complaints. It was like getting out of jail."

Ann turned to me, "He's right, we pretty much stopped that last week..... Could it be that love is just staying away from putting each other down? Can you base a relationship on that?"

Mark said, "Of course you can. No two people can agree on everything. Steer clear of the differences and things will work out. They sure did last week."

"Maybe, but only if the differences are minor. But what Ann came here for is not minor. For her, it's a very big deal. You keep telling her, `I love you.' She wants to know what you mean."

Ann said, "That's it. Sweeping the little differences under the rug is fine with me. Last week was okay but we really didn't solve anything...... I'm here with him to learn how to work the big things out."

"Okay, fine, but for just a minute, don't worry about why you're here. Try to figure out what you say, or I guess what you do, whenever you have any disagreement? The bigger the bone of contention, the more you do it."

Mark said, "Like I just said, put-downs, slurs, wise-cracks, snide remarks, we do it all the time. It's not just me, it's her, too."

Ann nodded in agreement, "If we do anything well, we're good at that. I push his buttons and he pushes mine."

"Okay, then, what do you actually do when you push those buttons?"

Mark said, "She's on my back all the time. She won't let up."

"I have to keep repeating myself because you tune me out. What about you? All you do is put everybody down. You know what's right for the whole world."

"How about your ultimatums? Your latest is saying you're leaving me if I don't marry you. How do you think that makes me feel?"

"How do you think I feel when you keep holding your brother's marriage over my head. You're not your brother. I'm not my sister, how many times do I have to tell you that?"

"See, there you go again."

"Getting in the last word, that's so important to him. Okay, be my guest, you can have it."

I said, "Sounds like you're really good at pushing each others' buttons. What do you do if you really get angry?"

"I know what she does. She holds back on sex, that's her way of getting back at me."

"How about the nights when you won't even touch me, when you pull away if I get too close to you in bed?"

I offered, "How about this? Do you think you could stop the button pushing? You pretty much did it for a week. Could you stop it for another week? Keep talking but be aware of what you're saying. When you have the urge to complain or put each other down, make an effort to say or do something positive instead."

Mark said, "I'm willing. I think I can do it for a week."

I said, "No matter what she does or says, you'll do it for a whole week."

Mark said, "No, you didn't say that. I'll do it for a whole week if she does it, too."

Ann said, "See, it's always up to me. It's all my fault that I want to get married. But I can keep my mouth shut for another week if you think it's going to help anything. But I'll tell you, Dr. Glasser, as much as we loved each other, we've bickered from the start. We almost broke up because we couldn't agree on the apartment. Bickering is a way of life for us..... But so what, everybody bickers, that's the way people are. So we ease up for a week, big deal. What's that going to solve?"

Mark said, "Ann's got a point. I've been living with bickering all my life. My parents bickered, they still do. My grandparents are past bickering, they don't even speak to each other. I really worry my brother and his wife are going to stop bickering and kill each other. The things they say, they don't care who's listening....... I feel sorry for their kids."

I said, "So you've argued about a lot of things, not just about when you should get married...... Am I right?"

Ann said, Of course you're right."

"But last week, did you do it?"

Mark thought for a moment and then said, "No, not really. It felt so good when she stopped complaining about my work and about the kids she has to teach. She did give me a few it's-time-we-get-married looks but it didn't bother me that much."

Ann said, "I guess we didn't disagree much about anything."

Mark nodded in agreement and they both looked for me to say something so I went on,

"Here's what I think you did last week. For a whole week, you avoided using the seven deadly habits that kill love and you had a better week than you've had in a long time. Those seven habits may be what has Mark so scared about getting married. He's seen what they do to marriages, he just described it."

Ann asked, "There are actually habits that kill love?"

"You'll recognize them as soon as I tell you. They're what you've been describing. And they're not going to be easy to get rid of. They not only cause the problems, but then, you use the same seven habits to deal with the problems they cause. It's a double whammy. That's what makes them so deadly. It's like starting a fire with gasoline and then throwing on more gasoline to put it out."

I paused for a moment for this to sink in.

"No matter what your partner says or does, for a loving relationship, you have to eliminate *criticizing, blaming, complaining, nagging, threatening and punishing*. And also get rid of the seventh, *bribing*, giving only if you get something. If you don't stop using them before you get married, you can save yourself a lot of misery if you'd kiss each other goodbye right now."

They were quiet for a long time. Then Ann said,

"What you're proposing is impossible. Suppose he comes home and tells me, `I can't stand my boss, I want to quit my job, we can live on your salary for a while.' Am I supposed to hug and kiss him and say he's wonderful? I'm putting up with all this traveling because he's convinced me he has a future there.... Or how about if he keeps his job and buys the Classic Porsche he wants that we can't afford."

Mark said, "You do a lot of things I don't like, too."

"Of course I do. That's what I mean. We've been using those habits forever. I can't see giving them up."

I said, "Of course you can't. The whole world has this problem. As soon as you have trouble with another person, those habits take over and love flies out the window."

Ann said, "When I have a legitimate beef, do I just turn the other cheek? I'm not a saint, I can't do that."

Mark said, "Yeah, it seems impossible...... But what can we do instead?"

"Okay, you asked a very good question..... What do you do instead? But before I try to explain, I wonder if you'd answer another question. Who can you always control?"

Mark said, "I don't know if this is what you're looking for but I guess the only person I can always control is myself. But when I get angry I have a hard time doing that."

I didn't say anything, I waited for Ann. She took a while and then said,

"What Mark said, I guess I can only control myself. I sure can't control him."

"So if you can only control yourself, have you ever succeeded in getting anybody to do what you want if they don't want to do it by criticizing or threatening them? This week was better because you didn't do that as much. You didn't argue, get angry, or withdraw to try to control each other. But have you ever done anything like this for much more than a week?"

Ann said, "Not me. I know when people try to control me, I resist. No one has the right to tell me how to live my life. Even my mother, what right has she to be so sure Mark is the man I should marry."

"Have you ever stopped trying to control someone important to you?"

"My mother, I've given up trying to make her stop nagging me about Mark. I just listen, I don't say anything. And I've just about made up my mind I'm going to stop trying to control Mark. It doesn't do a bit of good."

I said, "But that's just another way of sweeping it under the rug. You haven't solved anything. You've just clammed up."

"He's right, I clam up too. I do it all the time. There are a lot of things I don't talk about anymore like that Porsche you mentioned. Believe me, I still want it."

"Since you can't control anyone else and no one can control you, why do you both keep trying? Even clamming up becomes competitive, sort of like: I can clam up longer than you can."

Mark said, "It's all we know."

Ann said, "It's the way we are."

I said, "It may be all you know but it isn't the way you are. If it's the way you are, you haven't a prayer of finding love. For years now, you've both used these habits, they've harmed your relationship but you still kept using them..... Are you up to learning something better?" They nodded and I went on,

"Suppose I find a house I want to buy. The seller is asking a hundred thousand and I don't want to pay more than ninety. Do I start threatening him to try to force him to lower the price?"

Mark said, "I'm in sales, if I used any of those habits with a customer, I wouldn't sell a thing. In business, when we can't agree, we negotiate."

"How? What do you do?"

"Offer eighty and compromise at ninety."

I said, "The owner gives a little, You give a little and you're both satisfied, the deal works. Negotiating is something you can do instead of using the seven habits. Since you can only control yourself, you negotiate by saying what you will do to solve the problem, not what the other person should do or stop doing."

Ann said, "But in your example, neither of them got what they wanted, they had to settle for less. Marriage is the whole thing, you can't settle for less. That's what he's trying to get me to do now, settle for less, and it doesn't work for me."

I said, "That's a good point. There are things you can't negotiate and marriage is one of them. You can't be married and not married at the same time...... When you can't negotiate, then the only thing you can fall back on to solve the problem is love.... If you love each other, one will give in."

Ann said, "But who, which one gives in?"

Mark said, "Yeah, who?"

I said, "I don't know. No one can answer that question. But if you love each other one will. If neither of you will, what you have isn't love. But it's not that hard. Last week Ann gave in. She did it because she loves you. There's no other way to explain it."

Ann started to say, "But it was me, I gave..."

I interrupted, "I'm sorry Ann, there's more. If it's always the same person who gives in there's not much love. The closer it is to fifty-

fifty the more love you have. If the guy won't give in on the house it's no deal but you don't love that guy and you can always find another house. And if you don't love each other enough to sense when it's time to give in, you ought to start looking for someone else. Now is the time to make sure you have this kind of love, the kind that goes beyond negotiating, beyond giving up the seven habits."

Ann said, "Are you trying to tell me that what I did with Mark about his traveling was love, it wasn't a negotiation. Is that your definition of love?"

"I can't say it's my complete definition but I think it's an important part. But look, it's not what I think, it's what you think."

Ann said, "Mark, do you understand what Dr. Glasser just said? Do you agree?"

"All I know is when she gave in and stopped nagging me about my job it felt real good. I can't negotiate my traveling. They tell me to go and I've got to go. When she loved me enough to give in, I got some freedom and she got a lot more love from me."

"I did. But what's been such a pleasant surprise is I thought he'd just make more demands. But he hasn't."

Mark gave her a loving look and said,

"I appreciate what you did, I'm not about to ask for more."

I said, "When you use the habits, do they ever work?"

Mark said, "Sometimes they work for me. If I keep grinding on her long enough, she'll give in."

"But I get so resentful, I figure out a way to get back at him later."

Mark said, "But negotiating isn't that easy. It's hard to give up what you want when you want it real bad. Ann brought up that Porsche. I've stopped talking about it but I still want it. Where's the love if she says we can't afford it and won't give in?"

"I said, "If it's negotiable, go home and negotiate. If it's not, one or the other has to have enough love to give in. Listen to this tape, there's a lot on it. Talk about it. I'll be real interested in what you do this week. I hope you'll both be able to come next week.

Six

Ann and Mark had left feeling good and they were still in a good mood when they came back the following week. I started in by asking about the Porsche. Mark said,

"It's no problem, it turned out to be negotiable. We decided it'd be fun to look for one. To find out how much it'd cost. Then we can decide if we can afford it."

Ann said, "We're not rocket scientists but even we were able to figure out that we'd built up so much resentment by using the seven habits, we'd given up trying to negotiate."

Mark said, "Our week's been good. It's been a real effort but we've done a pretty good job of keeping the habits in check."

"I've got to agree with Mark. It was a good week. We cut down on using the habits, being aware of them really changes things and we really haven't had to negotiate that much. But I'm concerned. Eliminating the habits sounds too simple."

Mark said, "Getting rid of the habits is not simple and it certainly isn't easy. I've been listening to people at work all week. All I hear in our sales department is complaining, mostly about the customers and our boss but really about everything. And criticizing and blaming and threats about our quotas. I mean some days that's all I heard. And then when I called my brother I got a barrage from him about his wife. My God, if my brother and sister-in-law would learn this stuff, I think even they'd be able to get along."

"The same with my sister. She doesn't have a kind word for anyone, especially her daughter. Margo's a good kid but she can't seem to do anything to please my sister. She and my mother fight about her all the time. And about a lot of other things, too, all negotiable the way I see it. It was one or the other on the phone to me all week long. Those habits wreck everything."

They seemed to understand the habits and were working on getting rid of them so I thought it was time to get back on track. I said,

"Ann, last week I asked you about Mark saying, `I love you' all the time but then we never got very far with it. Could you say a little more about that?"

She thought for a moment,

"It's saying `I love you' after we argued. As if this is all I need to hear and I'll be happy."

Mark said, "But now that we're getting along so much better, I don't think she'll mind. Besides, I like to tell her I love her."

"You may like it but I don't..... The good news for me is you hardly said it last week."

I said, "But what irks you so much about him saying it?"

"It's hollow, the ring of a cracked bell. Saying I love you doesn't cut it for me anymore. People who love each other enough to live together for three years get married."

"Mark said, "But I do love you and I want to marry you. Especially now that we're understanding things more..... All I need is a little more time."

"See there he goes again, `I love you but I need more time.' Doctor, tell me how do you negotiate, `I need more time?' How much time is more time? I keep asking him and he won't tell me. I'm willing to negotiate but I have to know how much time he wants. Saying more is like saying nothing."

"Mark, I think Ann's got a point there."

Ann said, "More time is baloney as far as I'm concerned. Look, here's what I have to say and it isn't one of the habits. It's a straightforward statement. I may give up on Mark but I haven't given up on getting married and having a family."

I said, "Maybe Mark is trying to tell you that if you can give up using the habits on each other for a while, that'll be the time he needs. Mark, is that anywhere near what's on your mind?"

There was a long pause.

"See he doesn't answer you. He's afraid of marriage. He doesn't believe there is such a thing as a happy marriage."

Mark said, "No, not at all, I think a good marriage is difficult but it's possible. But Ann's right, I am afraid."

I said, "Ann, I think what Mark is trying to tell you is he doesn't see love as lasting very long. That's why him telling you over and over, `I love you.' rings hollow. Could the real message he's sending with those three words be, `I love you now but I'm not sure I'll love you long enough to marry you?'"

"That's not the message at all. What right do you have to put words in my mouth?"

"Mark, if that's not the real message, tell Ann what the real message is."

Ann looked right at him.

"Yeah, Mark, what's the real message?"

We both looked at him. This was not the time to back off. They were getting along. If he was ever going to answer that question, this was the time for him to do it.

"Okay, if it'll help, I'll stop telling her I love her. But it's hard. Those words are on my mind all the time. I thought women liked hearing them. I like it when she tells me she loves me."

But then I felt that maybe I was pushing him too hard. So I said,

"Look, I'm sorry. I'm not here to push anyone. But here's a question for both of you about love. How long do either of you think the way you feel now is going to last? What you honestly believe, not what you hope'll happen?"

This was an uncomfortable question. Neither of them wanted to be the first to express doubts about this good feeling lasting very long. Finally, Ann said,

"I've tried to avoid that question...... I mean I want it to last. And right now, if you told me I'd feel the way I felt for the last two weeks for a whole year, I'd be ecstatic...... But how can I help doubting love will last when I see relationships breaking up all around me. There are always a few teachers in my school on the verge of divorce. And the one's who are still together aren't that happy."

Mark said, "I couldn't say it any better than what she just said. I know she'd try hard if we got married, she's trying hard now. And you're right, I am afraid of the long haul...... But there are worse things than divorce, look at my whole family, all married and nobody's happy. To them the seven deadly habits are the ten commandments."

Ann said, "I think people who love each other their whole lives are an endangered species. They seem to be dying off all around us."

I said, "If you can't get rid of the deadly habits and learn to negotiate differences, no love will last. One or two cutting remarks and your relationship's in intensive care. But getting back to what I said last week, when you can't negotiate all you've got going for you is loving your partner enough to give in. In this situation, Mark'll have to give in and marry you or you'll have to give in and take a chance on never getting married. How you'll work this out will be the real test of your love. You can either be married or unmarried, you can't be both."

Mark said, "We can stay the way we are. The way we've been for two weeks. I'm sorry I even came in here today. All we have to do is keep loving each other, no one has to give in to anything."

I said, "Ann think about what Mark just said but before you answer tell me, at the worst point in your relationship, when you were fighting about getting married all the time, were you anywhere close to where your sister was when she got married to either husband. You were there, you know what they had going for them."

Mark said, "Go ahead Ann, tell him about your sister."

"Those marriages were doomed before they met each other. In the first one, she was sixteen years old and pregnant. The guy was a drunk and a druggie. But they got married because of the baby. He didn't work and now he's in jail. The second guy was better, he worked and he treated her okay. But they had nothing in common. They didn't share a single interest except sex. They had nothing to talk about except sports, the weather and spending money. He wanted her attention all the time and I think she still sees him once in a while because she's lonely."

"How about your brother and his wife, Mark? Do you think they're suited for each other? That if they'd treat each other better, they could make a go of it?"

"Maybe, but I doubt it. They're just two very different people. She was good looking and I guess for a while sex covered up their differences...... He's basically a loner with his nose in a book. She isn't happy unless she's with a group of people and the center of attention. Children or not, why they stay together is beyond me."

I said, "What got them together was sex. The same with Ann's sister both times. Hormones get people together but they don't keep people together. Do you think sex can keep people happily married for a life-time?"

Mark said, "I've been worried about that. But we've been together three years and the sex is still good. Great this past week."

Ann said, "Sex isn't our problem. It's been fine this past week....... But to me, that meant I had to keep my mouth shut about marriage...... If I didn't love him, the sex wouldn't keep us together...... But it does have something to do with why we're still together. I enjoy it with Mark because I love him. And idea of sleeping with other men, like it seems you have to today if you want to find someone, scares the hell out of me."

Mark said, "I think I see what you're driving at. You're talking about compatibility, aren't you? When Ann started saying she wasn't sure she wanted to marry me, I started to ask myself, `Are we compatible?' The first thing I looked at was sex and it was okay. It's better now but I didn't think we were having any trouble there. Then I looked at the things we like to do together. We both like to cook and to taste new foods. We like to eat out in ethnic restaurants and we enjoy talking about the food. A lot of living together has to do with food and here we're very compatible. (Ann nodded) Then we like to exercise, to hike and ride bikes. We used to argue about where to go but I think we're over that. We like movies, concerts and the theater and mostly we can afford to go. But what's most important is we're perfectly capable of entertaining ourselves. We can sit home and each do our own thing without being uncomfortable. She reads and I mess around on the net. And we both like kids, we spend time with Margo and my brother's kids. Their parents may be screwy but the kids are great. Maybe, we've been some help with them."

Ann said, "So sex is good and we're compatible, what happens next?"

"We get married. All I need is a little more time. The idea of locking myself into a marriage and a family, I'm still having trouble with that.... I'd like some more time the way we are now."

"Mark, that's exactly where we're incompatible. I look forward to locking myself into a loving marriage and family. Locking may be a bad word for you but it sound good to me. Marriage is a lot more than enjoying a bike ride or eating out in an interesting restaurant. I could do that with anyone. I see love as long-term, you don't. That's a huge incompatibility."

I said, "Ann, you don't have any concerns about locking yourself into marriage?"

"Of course, I have. I'm loaded with concerns but I've got a lot more concerns about where we are now. Pretending we're married when we're not....... Dr. Glasser, I wonder if we'll ever figure out what love is?

"We're working on it, I think we're making progress."

There was a pause after I said that as if neither of them agreed we'd been making progress. Then Ann said, with some finality in her voice,

"Well, I don't know if it's progress but right now I'm sure of one thing. Saying I love you is a cliche. I've heard it a thousand times, it means nothing to me. It's like meeting someone who asks, `How are you?' I always say, `Fine.' So what? It's meaningless. In the kind of relationship I want, love is more than talk, it's doing things to build a life together."

Mark said, "We've cut out trying to control each other and we had a great week. That's doing something to build a life together."

"No, Mark, that's not doing something, that's not what I'm talking about. All that is stopping doing things that hurt us. And that's good. But what I'm talking about is building a life together, to me that's what love is.

I said, "What do you think, Mark?"

"I tell her honestly, I need more time and she starts to push me. She's using these discussions to pressure me."

By asking him that question, I'd given Mark a real chance to take a step forward. But as usual, he changed the subject. Ann was so used to him doing this that she didn't even repeat the question. She just countered with,

"Mark, you asked to come here and talk. And it's done some good. We are getting along better. But if all you want now is more time, there's no sense you coming anymore."

"No, I want to come, I do..... But I have to tell you honestly...... honesty's a part of love isn't it? What I'm upset about is we're getting along and you won't let things be for a while. But as soon as I explain that, I can hear you saying, a while, tell me, Mark, how long is a while? As long as we're getting along so well, what's the difference how long it takes? We'll never get together if we don't keep doing what we're doing now. Why rock the boat? If we can keep doing what we're doing, the future will take care of itself."

Ann paused for a long time. What Mark said was sinking in. I couldn't tell exactly what she was feeling but I could see she was doing some serious thinking. After a few minutes she said in what seemed to me a very flat, almost resigned tone of voice,

"You really do like the way things are now. You do, don't you?"

I'd brought up the idea of compatibility and Mark answered it better than I thought he would. At an interest level they were very compatible, superficial compatibility was not the problem. The problem is after all this talk, Mark didn't trust love enough to marry her and she did. And after his little speech about the future taking care of itself it was becoming clear to Ann that after three years the future was here. It was the flat way she just said, `You really do like the way things are now,' that told the story. Ann was realizing that his giving up the habits was just another evasion of the real issue, marriage. I don't even think Mark heard the flatness in her voice. What he heard when she didn't mention marriage was she'd accepted his offer, stay the way we are and let the future take care of itself. Mark said,

"Don't you like it? How could you not like the way we've been for the past two weeks?"

There was another long pause. It was obvious Ann was struggling with whether to say something more about the status quo not being good enough. But then when she answered him I was surprised by the her voice. It had lost most of its flatness. It even had a little mock enthusiasm when she said just what he wanted to hear,

"I do, Mark. I like it a lot. We're doing great. It's good to see you so happy....... Anyway, I think it's time to go."

I thought it better not to comment on what she said or how she said it...... I gave them the tape and said, "I'm looking forward to seeing you next week."

Seven

Ann came in the following week without Mark, explaining that, at the last minute, he had to go out of town. She then said,

"I'm usually unhappy when he has to leave town but I was hoping he'd have to go. I was thinking about how I could possibly say what's been on my mind all week if he were here. But he's not and that's good. I wonder, do you remember I told you how good I felt that first year when we didn't ever want to be separated. I think I said, I was so in love I didn't even think about marriage." "I remember that."

"It's been a long time but all this week I've been trying to recapture that feeling. I've been asking myself, was I really in love that first year? Was Mark really in love? It seemed we were and, to tell you the truth, up to the last few weeks it still seemed we were.

But now I'm not so sure. Do you have any idea what I'm trying to tell you?"

"Last week, just before you left, something about love hit you. Your face lost expression and your voice turned flat. Mark was full of how wonderful the last few weeks had been; telling you to accept things the way they were, not to pressure him for more. Then you acted as if you agreed with him. But the way you did it told me you really weren't agreeing at all. But I don't think he noticed. All he heard was your agreement. I asked myself, why did she say she agreed? Instead of getting angry at his evasiveness, you seemed to accept it. Am I right? Is that what happened?"

"It is. You just described exactly what happened. I was hoping Mark'd notice but he didn't. He was happy all the way home that there'd be no more pressure. All week, I didn't even intimate anything about marriage and he was ecstatic."

Ann then stopped and just sat there thinking. I didn't say anything. I didn't even look at her. Sometimes, when a person's thinking real hard even a look can disturb an important train of thought. I just fiddled with some things on my desk. Finally she asked,

"Doctor Glasser, is it possible to be in love with love?"

I was careful here. She'd done a lot of thinking since our last session and seemed to be in the process of figuring something out. I didn't want to say anything that might interfere with the direction her thoughts were taking.

"Anything about love is possible. Tell me what you've been thinking about, even if it isn't clear."

"If it's possible to be in love with love, I think for the first year that's where we both were, more in love with love than with each other."

"Are you talking about infatuation?"

"We started out infatuated, everybody starts out infatuated. What we had became more than infatuation."

"I'm not sure I understand what you're driving at."

"That's how it began. Like I just said, everybody starts out infatuated. But infatuation doesn't last a year, I don't think it lasts much more than a couple of months. What I think was going on most of the first year was, we were both in love with love. I mean it's a feeling, a wonderful feeling. It's that feeling we were in love with. But I don't think we were in love with each other. We needed each other to get the feeling but I don't think that feeling is what you and I are searching for. I don't think that feeling is love. Is what I'm saying making any sense to you?"

"But what's the difference between infatuation and being in love with love? I'm not sure I see any difference."

"Infatuation is the chemistry, it's sexual. For a while I was infatuated with that math professor but I was never in love with him. That's why I got over him so quickly. It hurt but nothing like what I'm going through now. Mark and I had a lot of sex that first year but what we had was a lot more than infatuation. But it was after the first year, that's when I began to fall in love with him, that's where I am now. But it didn't happen for Mark. He continued to be in love with love. I don't think he's ever shifted over to being in love with me and I'm not sure he ever will. I want a man who's in love with me, not just in love with the feeling of being in love. Am I crazy or do you think I'm onto something?"

"You're onto something. It makes sense. It explains what's going on between you and Mark. I've got to hand it to you. It explains what happens between a lot of men and women in your situation, a long relationship but no marriage in sight."

"Last week I said, love is doing things to build a life together. It's more than getting rid of things like the habits. You asked Mark what he thought and he changed the subject. He has no clue what building a life together means. All he wants is to stay in love with love. Three years we've been together and that's where he still is. That's what hit me so hard at the end of last week's session. All week long I wondered, will he ever move from being in love with love to trusting my love enough to be in love with me?"

"Ann, I think you've already found that out. That was written all over your face at the end of last week's session."

"But I'm not sure. I may be wrong."

"Sure, you may be wrong. But what else can you do to find out than what you're doing? You can't make him fall in love with you. No one can do that. You did a lot to help each other fall in love with love. Lot's of people do that. That's the easy part, easy because it feels so good. And if it isn't going anywhere, it doesn't require that anything change. When Mark kept saying, `Let's not rock the boat,' you finally realized he doesn't want any more than to be in love with love and you're the one he's using to get that feeling."

Ann got a little angry, "Exactly, that's it. He is using me. No, not in a mean way, not trying to hurt me, but that's what's going on. And it does make me a little angry. What struck me is how satisfied he is with the way things are. Without the deadly habits things are better for him than they've been in a long time. Now it's so much easier for him to stay in love with love. If he married me now, he wouldn't make any more effort to build a life together than he's making now."

"Actually, I think he'd make less effort. Once you get married, I don't think it's possible to stay in love with love."

"What do you mean?"

"Because then you're restricted to one person. You either take the next step and fall in love with each other or you fall out of love with love and it's over. The whole fantasy of being in love with love needs another person for it to work but it doesn't have to be any particular person. I think you're right. Mark's not in love with you, he's in love with love and you're the person who makes the fantasy work for him."

"Why do you call it a fantasy?"

"It's a fantasy because it isn't real. Love is real, it takes two real people with real feelings for each other. Mark is a real person but his feelings for you aren't real. You saw that clearly at the end of last week's session. It's the playboy philosophy; you're his present playmate. Not just for a month, for three whole years. And as long as you're willing to hang in there and not ask for anything real like building a life together, you're just what he wants. Even more so because you've eased up on the habits. But wives aren't playmates who can be easily discarded if they can't do what it takes to help keep the fantasy going. Wives are reality, that's why he doesn't want to marry you. Look around, you see yourself and Mark all over the place, couples happy until they get where you are or, worse, get married. Then, the wife wants more, a family, a home and the fantasy of being in love with love quickly falls apart. And with it, the relationship. Why should you be any different from them? Mark's sent a million `this is all I want, why rock the boat,' signals. It's not like he's tried to keep it secret."

Ann thought for a long time. Tears came into her eyes. When you're filled with love for someone it seems impossible he doesn't both love you and want what you want. Ann was finding this out and there wasn't anything she could do about it.

She said, "I think you're right. Honestly, I think, marrying Mark'd be a disaster."

I said, "My guess is a lot of women find out on their honeymoon that they married a man who was only in love with love."

"Why do you say women? Don't you think it happens to men, too?"

"It may, but today, with so many couples living together, it's rarely the men who are dying to get married. Women seem to make the transition to being in love with the person, many men find it more difficult."

Ann said, "I'm a woman, I don't know how men feel. I don't even know exactly how other women feel. All I know is how I feel. And I know Mark isn't in love with me. He thinks he is but he isn't. He's sincere when he says he loves me because he hasn't the vaguest idea it's the fantasy of love he's in love with, not me."

I tried to help her to a softer landing by saying,

"Maybe you could explain all this to Mark. He's not stupid, he might be in love with you; we really don't know."

"Please, don't try to make it easier for me. After three years you know I'm right. It's too late for us. It's gone on too long..... He's even less in love with me now than I hoped, not more. The way I see it there's a natural progression of love. Love can't stand still. It goes from being in love with love to being in love with each other, to getting married, to having children and being in love as a family. That's not going to happen with Mark and me."

"Are you still in love with him?"

"I am, that's the hell of it. Just because I've figured all this out, doesn't change my feelings about him. I still love him."

"So where do you go from here?"

"I don't know.... Breaking up after all this time is hard for me to imagine. He doesn't know he's in love with love. All he knows is: keep things the way they are, that's the only way he can hang on to that feeling. As long as I'm willing to go along with that, he's fine."

"You're going to give up on marrying him?"

"Unless he can give me a good reason not to. I've been hoping for too long....... I've got to stop hoping and trust my own instincts..........."

"Then she broke down,

"But without Mark, I don't even feel like living....... This has been a disaster. I should never have come here. I was better off not knowing. I really was. My God, what do I do now? I feel awful."

She hurried to the restroom, tears streaming down her face. And I had that same thought, `What do I do now?' But I don't believe it's as much a disaster as she thinks it is at this moment. It's been painful but she's learned a lot about love. It would've been a lot more painful if she'd discovered this after they were married. I just sat there waiting for her to come back. After about five minutes, she walked in and sat down with a sigh.

"Look, you'll just have to accept my crying. I'm so sad. I feel devastated. I don't think he's ever really loved me, I don't think he ever will."

Then I got an idea. It might not work but maybe it could help her move to a more positive way of looking at this situation. I said,

"Do you think you're unlovable? That Mark's the only man who'll ever love you? Can't there be anyone else?"

When I said that she started to cry harder.

"No, no, I'm not unlovable. I'm crying because I am lovable... I'm very lovable. And I'm loving, too. He'll never find anyone who loves him as much as I do."

I thought, that's good, she's not blaming herself.

"Ann, doing what we're trying to do is tough. But not doing it would be worse. Three years is a long time but women in your situation hang on for a lot longer hoping for a marriage that is very likely to be a mistake. Of course, you feel terrible but you've at least learned something these women don't know. You're not married, the door is open. You can escape."

"But I'm still with Mark. And I still love him. What do I do tonight when I go home. He thinks he loves me. What do I say? He won't understand what we've been talking about. I know he won't."

"Don't say anything. Take this tape and share it with him. Last week he said, honesty was important to him. So be honest. Let him hear you say that for you love is a progression that has an outcome. It's more than just a feeling. You owe it to him to do this. You owe it to yourself...."

"I guess you're right. God, I'm exhausted. I never expected anything like this to happen to me."

"I didn't expect this either. I think you've come up with something important. If it weren't, you wouldn't be so upset. The idea of you and Mark living happily ever after is hard to give up. I can see that. But Ann, I think you're a very strong woman, a weaker person would never have figured this out. Give yourself some credit and some time, you're going to work this out. You don't have to do it today. You don't even have to play that tape for Mark when you go home if you don't feel like it.

"I guess there's nothing more for us to do today."

"The time's almost up anyway......... Ann, I'm sorry to tell you this when you're so upset but I have a lecture tour coming up, I won't be

27 - 07 - 19~ 2004

WILLIAM GLASSER INSTITUTE
IN IRELAND (WGII)

Received from _____ Ann Grey _____ n of

_____ What is Reality Called Lords Chait Talk _____

_____ Twenty eight euro. _____

Deposit ☐

Paid in full ☐

Balance due

£ _28-00_ . Signed _____

№ 5686

here for the next two weeks. That makes our next meeting Thursday, three weeks from today. Talk with Mark if you're up to it. And try to listen to what he has to say. Just don't do anything drastic."

Ann's a competent person. She'll live through this. The math teacher in her will be happy she solved the problem even though the solution is painful.

Eight

When I got back on Sunday from my lecture tour, there was an urgent call from Mark waiting on my machine. He was upset. He wanted to see me by himself. I got in touch with him on Monday at his office, he'd given me his work number, I explained,

"Mark, I've got a little problem with seeing you by yourself if you're upset about what's going on with Ann. You see, I'm not sure you understand why I'm seeing her. Do you know why she and I are having these meetings?"

"Sure, I know why you're seeing her. She's upset because I won't marry her right away. I need some more time, that's what we've been talking about."

"No, that's really not it. I didn't think you were paying much attention to the real reason. Our meetings were set up to help her figure out what love is. It's been difficult and she's having a hard time with what she's been learning. She was crying when she left here last time. I'm not surprised if she's still upset."

"But it's because she's so upset that I want to see you. I love her, I hate to see her this way. I want to help."

"That's reasonable, but I want to make it perfectly clear I won't see you as a client. I'll only see you if Ann believes that seeing you by yourself will help her learn more about love. Talk it over and if it's okay with her I'll meet with you. It's up to her to make that decision."

Mark agreed and must have gotten in touch with Ann at school because a little later that day she left a message on my machine that it was fine with her if Mark wanted to see me. Mark called and we made an appointment for Tuesday. Ann had mentioned in her message that she was looking forward to seeing me at our regular time on Thursday.

When Mark came in he looked terrible, as if he'd hardly slept. It was obvious that Ann wasn't the only one upset. Before he could say anything I said,

"Mark, I want to tape this conversation just like I've been taping all the conversations. I'll give you the tape but it's up to you if you want to share it with Ann. But I'm not going to keep it a secret. If Ann calls, I'm going to tell her it was taped. Also, on Thursday, if she asks me what we talked about I'm going to tell her. What we talk about is not confidential. Don't say anything you wouldn't want her to hear."

"Doctor, it's fine. Tape it. And if she wants to hear it I'll be happy to play it for her. All I want to do is help her and I'm at my wit's end. I don't know what's going on. She isn't the same Ann. I've never seen her like this, I don't think I've ever seen anyone like this.... I'm scared. What's happened to her?"

I nodded for him to go on,

"She's so sad. I think it's even more than sad. She's depressed. I mean almost all the time. She starts to cry right in the middle of anything we're talking about. When I wake up at night, her pillow's soaking wet, I don't know how long she's been crying. I keep asking her what she wants me to do and she says, `Do whatever you want. I'm not going to tell you what to do.' She seems to be able to handle work but she admits it's hard. It's like waves of sadness hit her and she has to cry. I told her to get some Prozac, half the people I work with are on it. But she said to me, `I don't want drugs. I have a right to be sad. I'm not telling you what to do, please don't tell me what to do.' Doctor, if this keeps up I may ask you for some Prozac for myself."

I disregarded his comments about Prozac, neither of them are in therapy with me. And there's nothing abnormal about their upset. It would be abnormal for them not to be upset in this situation. I said,

"Did she play the tape of our last meeting for you?"

"Three times. We listened to it together every time. I still don't understand it, she's in love with me, I'm in love with love. What kind of nonsense is that? I'm miserable, she's miserable. She knows I love her. I love her very much."

"What do you want me to do?"

"Help us, I can't go on like this. She's close to falling apart. I haven't had a good night's sleep since we played that tape. We were getting along so well and now this. Why? What's suddenly gone wrong?"

"I'm not sure if this is going to help you but I think she's getting close to understanding what love is..... She's having a hard time dealing with it...... Does anything you say seem to cheer her up?"

"Nothing I say helps. As soon as I start to ask her, what's going on, she starts to cry. Keeping my mouth shut is the only thing that seems to help. But it's so hard to do. I mean I'm living with someone I've never known. Someone I don't want to know. She's always been such an upbeat person. Doctor, please, what should I do?"

"Maybe it's time you find out what she's been learning."

"Find out what? I know what love is. It's what I feel for Ann. What more is there?"

"Mark, love may be a little more than what *you* feel. It has to do with what she feels, too."

"Oh, yeah, I'm sorry, I forgot. It takes two to be in love, I know that. But she's in love with me, she said so on the tape."

I took note of that omission. Like a lot of men and women, too, Mark believes that if he's in love with someone, that someone has to be in love with him. But what seems to count with him is much more his feeling than hers.

"Does she seem to be in love with you right now? That tape you mentioned is three weeks old."

"Sure she's in love with me, that's what's got her so upset. But you've got her all mixed up. Like she said on that tape, `I should never have come here.' I say amen to that."

"I don't think she's mixed up at all. I think she's disappointed with the way things have worked out with you. What she said on the tape is she's in love with you but you're not in love with her. You're in love with love. If you listened to the tape, it was clear that she figured that out herself. I agreed with her but I didn't put that idea in her head. Do you have any idea what she means when she says you're not in love with her, you're in love with love?"

"I think it's some kind of a crazy idea that she figured out because she's been seeing a psychiatrist. It's seeing you that has her all mixed up..... But look, I'm here to help her. Tell me what you think she means when she says, I'm not in love with her, I'm in love with love?"

"It's hard to explain, but I'll try...... Tell me, why do you want a Porsche so much?"

"I think most guys want a Porsche. When you're driving around in a Porsche, it feels great. A friend of mine has one. He let's me drive it. I love that feeling. Ann knows how I feel about a Porsche. She wants me to have one someday, we talked about that."

"Can it be any Porsche or is there a particular Porsche that you want above all other Porsches?

"Oh, I guess there are a few great Porsches but any Porsche in mint condition, even an old one, would be good enough for me. But what does me wanting a Porsche have to do with loving Ann? Why are we talking about Porsches?"

"Please, give me a minute more.... If you got a Porsche like you wanted would that be good enough for you forever or might you want to get a better one some day? Or maybe a Jag or a vintage Mustang?"

"Doc, a Porsche is only a car. Nobody wants a car forever. If they did, the whole auto industry'd go broke."

"So it's not any particular car that you'd want forever. What you want forever is the feeling you get when you're behind the wheel of a great car. Cars are going to come and go all your life. It's the good feeling that comes with a new car that keeps the auto industry in business. If it weren't for the feeling that goes with getting something you want, the whole country'd go broke."

"Okay, I'd like a Porsche. What's this got to do with Ann and me?"

"Mark, Ann's willing to take a chance that her feeling for you will last and grow if you get married and begin to build a life together. She doesn't want a new man or any man in mint condition. She wants you for ever and ever."

"I know that, that's what I've been trying to tell you."

"But what's got her so concerned is she's figured out that you're in love with the feeling of being in love. You're getting that feeling now with her. But you're not convinced you need her to get that feeling. It's like buying a new car, you can always trade it in for newer model to keep that good feeling alive. You're worried if you marry Ann the feeling may go away and you don't want to take a chance on that. If you were in love with her, not just the good feeling, you wouldn't be worried about marriage."

"How can I not be worried? For years we've been doing so well, why rock the boat? I think everyone's in love with love. It's not just me, it's her, too."

"Maybe she was in the beginning but not now. It's you she loves, she isn't worried about rocking the boat. She's worried you don't love her enough to marry her. You're not in love with her like she is with you. Do you understand what I'm trying to explain?"

"Look, I don't get it. I'm in love with her. I want to marry her. I just want to be sure. Can you blame me for being cautious?"

"Ann doesn't think you're ever going to be sure. She thinks that after all this time you're as sure as you're ever going to be and that's not sure enough for her. She doesn't want to give you any more time. Personally, I think you've done her a favor by holding off on asking her to marry you. It's given her a chance to figure all this out."

Mark completely ignored what I just said.

"But I'm still worried about Ann. That's what I came in here for. All we have to do is go back to where we were when we got rid of the seven habits and we'd both be fine."

"Mark, you are back where you were when you got rid of the seven habits. It just took her a little time to realize it."

"How can you say that? We were happy and now we're miserable?"

"When you say we were happy, do you mean both of you or just you?"

"Both of us, you saw how happy we were when we came in here."

"I didn't see it the last time you were here together. At the end of our session, she was very unhappy. We talked about that on the tape, you heard it. She realized you were not in love with her when you wouldn't do anymore than say, `I love you. Let's leave well enough alone.' It may be well enough for you but it isn't for her. She's been trying to resign herself to the fact that you don't really love her. It hurts Mark, you've just told me how much she's hurting. But she'll get over it. Women do it every day."

"But I do love her. If I didn't love her, would I be this upset? And she loves me."

"Mark, you're right. She still loves you but she feels her love for you is running out of time, that's why she's so upset."

"What are you talking about it's running out of time? It hasn't run out. I can feel she still loves me."

"I agree, it hasn't run out, yet."

"Then please, tell me what she wants?"

"She wants you to marry her.... now. I don't think she'll live with you much longer unless you do. For a long time she tried to deny how important getting married was to her but she can't do it anymore. It was toward the end of our last session when she started to cry. That's when it hit her. I really don't know what she's going to do now. I think for a while she'll just keep crying."

"But that's pressure. Do you think if I let her pressure me into marriage, we could be happy?"

"Mark, I don't think she can pressure you into marriage. If you marry her now after all we've talked about today, it'll be because you love her. You understand what I've been explaining to you. Apart from marrying her, there's nothing else you can do."

"So you're saying I should marry her?"

"Absolutely not. I'm telling you that's what she wants. Personally, I think you're still in love with love. I don't think she should marry you now even if you asked her. But it's not up to me, it's up to you and her."

"But on that tape she said she'd marry me if I asked her."

"Like I just said, it's not up to me."

"She thinks things'll work out if I made up my mind and married her. She's said that a lot."

"Then don't listen to me, go ahead and ask her. That's the only way you'll find out..... Look Mark, we're going around in circles...... But don't fret. You're in good company. Lot's of men are living with women who desperately want to get married and they won't marry them because they're only in love with love. Being in love with love fools you. You believe you're in love with her and I think at times you're just as puzzled as to why you won't marry her as she was before she figured out what was going on. You're using her to get the feeling. You heard Ann say that on the tape."

"You're wrong. I'm not using her. I love her. I don't believe any of that in love with love crap. I'm just not ready to marry her yet. I can't explain why, I'm just not."

"That's the most honest thing you've said since I met you. I hope you play this tape for her, she should hear you say it."

"I'm scared to play the tape. I don't know what she'll do. She may try to kill herself."

"You're a good man Mark but I don't think she'll kill herself over you. I think if you'll play this tape for her you'll be doing both of you a big favor."

"But what's going to happen to me?"

"I don't know. But if you'd just said, what's going to happen to us instead of what's going to happen to me, I think you'd be getting closer to what love is. Maybe you'll meet a woman who'll settle for what you're willing to give. God knows they're out there."

Mark left shaking his head. He just couldn't conceive that marriage could be that important to Ann when he enjoyed being in love with love so much. I'd come right out and told him what was going on and what she wanted and he turned it down. But unless she actually separates from him, he's not about to disappear from her life. He'll keep playing "I love you" games with her. All men and women who are in love with love play these games. It helps them to avoid the feeling that the relationship is standing still. The excitement of coming closer then pushing away, the fighting and making up, the will I or won't I, should I or shouldn't I, games. What they are doing is running in place - a lot of movement but going nowhere. Ann's discovered that real love doesn't stand still. It always has a destination and it moves in that direction. If it stands still too long, like water, it stagnates.

*****

Ann called me almost as soon as Mark left. I picked up the phone myself because I knew it was her. She was hoping I'd worked a miracle and Mark would come home ready to get married. I said,

"I saw Mark, we had a good talk. He has the tape, ask him to play it for you."

"He's not going to marry me."

"Ann, please, only Mark knows that. Ask him to play the tape.

There was a long pause. I heard her put the phone down. Then she yelled at it from a distance telling me to wait a minute. I guess she must've been on her way to get a tissue. It was several minutes before she came back. She seemed to have pulled herself together a little and asked,

"What do I do now?"

"Keep crying if you feel like it. The tears will protect you, don't try to shut them off. If you feel like crying in front of your students, cry. Tell them the truth, you've got problems with a guy. They'll love you for it. Students need to know their teacher has a life, they'll want to help.... And Ann, there's some more about love I'd like to talk with you about on Thursday. I think it can help you with what's happening now.

Nine

I was surprised at how much better Ann looked when she came in on Thursday, much better than I expected. So much so that I didn't even ask her how she felt. Instead, I asked,

"How's Mark been doing since he saw me Tuesday,"

"Not very well. He really wanted to come today but he couldn't get the time off. He told me to be sure to bring the tape home.... Anyway, after you told me to cry any time I felt like it, I've been feeling a little better. Was that some kind of a trick?"

"No, trick, just a little bit of free therapy..... It gave you a little more control over the situation than you thought you had. It's part of that choice theory I talked about when you first heard me."

"Anyway, as soon as Mark saw how much better I'm doing, he got real down. He's beginning to realize I'm not kidding. I think he's terrified I'm going to tell him to leave. He keeps saying he can't live without me. He's almost as tearful as I was. I can't help it but I'm feeling guilty. Do you think I'm being too hard on him?"

"Ann, if you're going to leave him there's no easy way to do it. But it's not going to be as hard on him as it's been on you. You've had some rough weeks. Of course, you're upset when you see him crying. You love him. For him to be happy, all you'd have to do is give up on marriage and go back to the way you were. You know that... If you leave him, once in a while, months, even years later, when you think of Mark, don't be surprised if you have a moment or two of sadness. You're going through a painful time. There's no way to avoid it."

"It's harder for me because I'm in love with him and he's only in love with love, is that it?"

"Much harder. You know that. You're much more replaceable for him than he is for you. If he was in love with you, he'd stop crying and marry you. It's as simple as that."

But I never thought it'd be so painful."

"But you said, the past two days have been better."

"Better for me maybe, but worse for Mark. I hate seeing him this miserable."

"Ann, you love him but you have no control over anything he does or he feels. That's up to him. But while you're going through this I've been wondering, is there a less painful way to break up with someone you still love? Does it always have to hurt so much?"

"I know how I feel, totally rejected and betrayed."

"I don't think there's anyway to avoid the way you feel. But if Mark won't marry you, Ann, you're going to breakup. It may drag on for a while longer but it's going to happen. Can you think of anything you can do to make it less painful?"

"You believe I can do something in this horrible situation?"

"I think it's worth considering."

"You have an idea or you wouldn't have brought it up."

"Ann, did you ever have a large piece of adhesive tape on a cut and had to pull it off? How did you do it? Or go for a swim in an icy pool. How did you go in?"

"I know how I should do it. But I don't always do it that way."

"You're no different from most people but how should you do it?"

Pull it off quickly, dive in, why prolong the misery?...... I guess that's what you're trying to tell me."

"If you care about Mark, once you've made a decision to break up, you shouldn't prolong it. I'm not sure you've made that decision yet but if you make it, break clean and quick. It may hurt more than what you're doing now but not for nearly as long. I think another thing to learn about love is to end it when it's over. What you're doing now hurts. You hurt, he hurts. It's Chinese Water Torture."

"But how quick is quick, a week, a month?"

"I think a couple of weeks, if he wants another week, I'd give it to him. What's another week? It's been three years. Quick to me is no more than a month. But that's me, do what makes sense to you."

"But I've got to give him time to find a place."

"I guess this means your plan is to stay in the apartment?"

"I've put a lot of work into that apartment. And money, too. It's more my place than his. I have no intention of moving out. There are still six months left on our lease. I'll take his name off the lease if he wants me to. I don't plan to move."

"What if he won't go?"

"He'll go. He won't give me a hard time, that's not Mark's way. We've never talked about it but all along I felt that was the plan if we ever broke up."

"But as soon as you give him a time to get out, two weeks, maybe three weeks, what if he asks you to marry him? You still love him, what are you going to do?"

"I don't know. I want to marry him. If he asks me, do you think we should get couples' counseling?"

"I can't say not to but I have my doubts. Just by asking that question shows you're unsure of Mark. If he were really interested, it might be worth a try but not for more than a few sessions. It could end up as another way to drag things out. You have to be very careful of getting into any situation that would prolong the misery. You could be setting yourself up for a five year engagement... What could you say if he asks you to marry him that would be loving and still protect you, really protect both of you?"

"I see your point, we'd have to set a date."

"Okay, I'll play Mark and ask you to marry me, *Ann I love you and I want to marry you?* What would you do?"

"I'd hug and kiss him. We'd both cry for a while but for me it'd be tears of joy. But right then, I'd tell him, I'll go along with whatever you want as long as it's right away. Personally, I'd like a wedding but a judge at city hall would be fine."

"How much time are you thinking of?"

"Two months, I'm not willing to wait more than two months."

"Okay, here's another question, if you separate and after a few months he asks you to marry him, would you do anything differently?"

"No, as long as I was unattached, I'd do the same thing."

"Are you going to start looking for someone else as soon as you separate."

"I don't know. I don't think I'll look but if someone comes along, I'll see him. I'm upset but grieving's not my style. But I'm never going through anything like this again. This is more like a divorce than a breakup. For all practical purposes, it's been like a marriage for the last three years. One thing I know, I don't want another man in love with love. One's enough for me."

"Will you consider seeing Mark after he moves out?"

"Yes, as long as I still love him and want to marry him. The ball's still in his court until I find someone else. Oh, that's another thing we do, play tennis. I'll be more than happy to keep playing tennis with him or go to the theater with him. But he's not going to stay over, not even one night."

"How about sex?"

"No, I don't think that'd work for me."

"You've really been doing a lot of thinking."

"I can suffer and plan at the same time. For me, I think they kind of go together. But I'll tell you, I also know that I may blow the whole thing. I still love him, what I've been telling you may be all talk."

"This is a good time to bring up another point about love. It may help you to separate from Mark and not hurt so much. You're in love with him. Are you in love with anyone else?"

"Of course not. Well, you know I love my family, we talked about that."

"No, someone a lot closer than your family."

"I give up, tell me?"

"I think we all need to be in love with ourselves. By that I mean, to take care of ourselves. That doesn't mean we can't love others, sometimes loving ourselves helps us to love others."

"You're right about that. I loved Mark and I thought if I loved him enough he'd marry me. But then I think, maybe I didn't love him enough. When I think that, I feel terrible about myself. I start blaming myself. But that's not right. I'm just hurting myself."

"That's what I mean. You need to love yourself to get over Mark. It's protective. Look at some of the kids who are flunking in your classes, how do you think they feel about themselves."

"Those kids feel terrible, failure is terrible. A lot of them hate themselves. They go out of their way to screw up their lives....... Like I'd be doing if I hung on to Mark. I'd be hating myself, wouldn't I?"

"When you love yourself, you take good care of yourself. You don't use the seven deadly habits on yourself. You try not to use them on anyone."

"What do you mean?"

"You don't criticize yourself or blame yourself. You don't spend time tearing yourself down when things don't go well. You've known for years that you and Mark might be headed for where you are now and what were you doing to yourself?"

"I was just hanging on hoping. I thought a lot about the problem but I never really faced it."

"Do you think you're getting close to facing it now?"

"I'll know more after I play this tape to Mark. I'd like to tell you how strong I am, how I understand love a lot better now but I can't. I'm not as sure as I sound. I feel strong in here talking to you, but not nearly so strong when I have to deal with Mark. I keep thinking I may be doing something very wrong."

"Ann, that's my point. It's so easy to criticize yourself when things don't go right, you're always available to yourself. You always hurt yourself when you do that. And in a way, you hurt Mark too by not being strong enough to take a stand. If you come to the conclusion that the life you want is not going to happen with Mark, you owe it to yourself to find a better life. Keep your mind open and listen to Mark. But it's not up to you to take care of him. It's up to him to take care of himself. It's not your job to build him up or tear him down. But it's especially important that you don't tear yourself down.... Remember, you can get away from people who criticize you but you can never get away from yourself...... Okay? Here's the tape. You ought to have an interesting week. If Mark wants to come next time it's fine with me. But it's really up to you."

Ten

It was hard to tell the mood they were in when Ann and Mark arrived for our meeting. I greeted them and waited for one of them to begin. Mark started by saying,

"I think this whole thing is unfair. I'm being ganged up on. No one really cares how I feel. Three years and now this, get out in a few weeks. She keeps talking about love but what's kicking me out have to do with love?"

Ann listened patiently to Mark's complaints and said,

"It seemed so easy to move in together but now I can see it was a terrible mistake. But it's done and we're where we are right now. Mark, for the final time, tell me your solution? I've given you mine. I've told you what I plan to do. That was crystal clear on the tape and I haven't changed my mind. This is your chance to tell me what you can do right now that's better. And please don't say, go back to the way we were. That's telling me what I should do. I'm not interested in hearing you tell me what I should do. I've finally figured that out. Tell me what you'll do, you not me."

Mark looked at her for a long time. Finally he said,

"But we're a couple Ann, it's not what you should do or I should do, it's what we should do."

"But that's just it, we're not my idea of a couple anymore. A couple gets married if they want to build a life together. I have to look out for myself and you have to look out for yourself. You heard the tape when Dr. Glasser and I talked about needing to love ourselves. This year I've begun to hate myself, not you. I don't enjoy separating but I'm beginning to feel a lot better about myself."

"Ann, if I'd marry you, then it would be okay? That's what you said on the tape."

"Maybe if you'd said it when I came home from here last week. But not anymore. Dr. Glasser, remember last week I said I still loved Mark and I'd marry him if he asked. Well, I don't feel that way right now. I said I believe love is a progression, that it has goals along the way. Like one goal is to get married. But goals have to be connected to time. I feel like we've been planning to build a home that's never going to be built, planning a trip we're never going to take. For me, marriage is a goal, a very important goal. I'm not ashamed to say I want to get married to a man I love who wants to marry me. I'm not one of those women who are so disillusioned with love that they don't even want to admit they want to get married. But the time for marrying Mark has run out. It's sad, God knows I've cried a lot about it. But I think it has."

"But it's your fault it has. It's not mine."

"I don't think it makes a bit of difference who's fault it is. If you want, I'll take the blame. If people ask you, tell them it's my fault, I won't deny it. Besides, you're probably right. It is my fault. You didn't force me to move in with you, that was my mistake, not your's. But you're not going to force me to stay with you, either. I take complete responsibility for us separating. But like on the tape, no long drawn out separation. No going back and forth to save something time's run out on. Rip the bandage off, no Chinese water torture."

"But you wanted to marry me. That's what started this whole thing."

"Are you asking me to marry you, right now, in front of Doctor Glasser, is this what I'm hearing?"

"Well maybe I am."

"Mark, this isn't how I want to be asked. Not when you feel I'm putting pressure on you. I haven't totally given up on the idea of marrying you but not before we separate for a while. Then if we see each other and get along, you figure out a way to ask me that makes me believe you really want to marry me, that there's no pressure on you to do it. And there's no pressure on me to accept your offer. I don't think we can go back to square one. But before I'd have any interest in marrying you, we'd have to be away from all this pressure."

I said, "Ann, I like your idea that love doesn't just go on and on as it is forever. It evolves. It has goals. But aren't the goals different for men and women your age?"

Mark said, "What do you mean?"

"I mean suppose you were both fifty years old. Would it have made much difference to either of you whether or not you got married?"

Ann said, "You're talking about my biological clock, aren't you? If my goal is to have a family, I can't afford to wait till I'm fifty."

"But you're only twenty seven, I'm twenty nine, we've got plenty of time."

Ann said, "The biology's important but it's more than that. Marriage for me is a lot more than having children. I've played at being married for three years and I've never liked it. I want to be a wife, not a woman living with a man. There isn't even a name for me in the English language. I'm a displaced person, a non-entity. Fifty years old or eighty years old, if I ever live with a man again he's going to be my husband. Or I'm totally sure he will be in a year."

Mark said, "You can never be totally sure."

"That's right, you can't. Right now, I have no intention of living with anyone again without being married. I may change my mind, but never for more than a year."

I said, "I wonder, is it different for you, Mark? Would you move in with a woman again after this experience?"

"Of course I would. I wouldn't even think of marrying Ann if I hadn't lived with her all this time. I don't understand how separating is ever going to get us together. Staying together is still our best chance."

"Mark, I don't think we have much of a chance. The more you talk the less I think we have. I'm finally ready to admit that love between a man and a woman must have a future. And for me that future is marriage. The funny part is I have a feeling that the next woman you live with you're going to marry. I've seen that happen often enough to know what I'm talking about."

"I don't want to cut you off but this ground has been thoroughly covered. Is there anything else you want to talk about or any questions you want to ask me?"

Mark said, "But what are we going to do? Do I have to move out right away?"

"Mark, Ann came here to discover what love is, not for help with her life. What you do from here on is up to you and Ann to work out.

It's not up to me to tell you what to do. If you want, I'll be glad to refer you to another therapist."

"Are you going to keep seeing Ann?"

"As long as she wants to continue to talk about the meaning of love. That was our deal. I think there are still some things we can learn. From what I gather she's going to be searching for a relationship she believes will lead to marriage."

Ann said, "Do you want me to come next week?"

"No, not next week. You have a lot to work out if you're going to separate from Mark. When you finish that, I'd like for us to start meeting again. Call me when you think you're ready. But take my advice, relax. The world isn't going to come to an end. You're both young, your lives are hardly over. A year from now, there's a good chance you'll both be doing well. And no matter what happens, I hope both of you use what we've learned so far. I think it'll help.

Eleven

I hadn't heard anything from Ann for three months, then I received the following letter.

Dear Dr. Glasser:

I've had more time on my hands than I'd hoped for since Mark moved out so please forgive this long letter. The good news is he moved out quickly, just three weeks after we last met. So far he's called four times to inquire if I'd changed my mind but still no mention of marriage. We talked for two hours the first time, an hour the second time and only about fifteen minutes the third and fourth times. He wanted to know if I've been going out and I told him, no, it was too soon. But I'm definitely interested. I've put the word out and I've had a few calls. By the time you read this I may have already had a date. One of the guys who called sounded interesting.

Incidentally, I've also had time to read your book, *Choice Theory.* I can see now exactly what you were trying to teach me. I guess the hardest part of being separated from Mark is the loneliness. Your claim that the need for love is built into our genes is right on target. Mark may have been more in love with love than he was with me but, in his own way, he still loves me. It's reassuring that he hasn't replaced me yet. And I have to admit I'm tempted to go back, but so far only tempted. But the good thing is I continue to feel better about myself than I did when I was with him and that's what gives me the strength to resist going back. Your explanation of the need to love ourselves was also right.

It was late at night, right after I read your description of the quality world in Chapter Three, that I got to thinking about the very first time I knew I wanted to be a bride. That long ago experience is still crystal clear in my mind as a cherished memory or, in your words, a picture in my quality world. It happened years ago, actually when I was a little girl just nine years old.

My grandma took me with her on a trip back East. We stayed at her sister Ella's house in Vevay, Indiana. Ella's daughter, Marian, was getting married and Grandma was invited to the wedding. It was springtime and all the trees were in blossom. You could even smell them. I still remember that sweet scent as we drove up to the house and how pretty Aunt Ella's garden was. She had a large front porch and a lovely big back yard. We all went to the wedding the day after Grandma and I arrived. This was the first wedding I'd ever been to. And I knew I'd never forget how beautiful it was.

The bride, in a huge puff of white silk organza and lace looked, to me, like an angel from heaven. She had seven beautiful bridesmaids each one wearing a different color, long billowy dress. They looked like spring flowers in petal pink, pale orchid, buttercup yellow, apricot, light green, periwinkle and lilac with matching hats. Each one carried white daisies, pink roses and violets in round bouquets with long ribbons streaming from them to match their dresses. To me it all seemed like a magical fairy tale. If you don't understand all this, ask your wife to explain it to you.

The next morning I woke up after dreaming all night about bridesmaids twirling to romantic music and the bride and groom waving from their regal places high atop an elaborate cake. Grandma told me to put a small piece of wedding cake under my pillow for good luck but I ate it before I fell asleep. I figured there was no sense squashing good cake. I went outside to play in Aunt Ella's backyard after breakfast. She had an orchard of peach trees in blossom at the end of her property near the fence. Aunt Ella told me that section of the yard used to be a victory garden during the war. Her father had planted all those trees and over the years they'd canned a jillion peaches in Mason Jars.

When I stood under the trees my head was completely surrounded by branches filled with the prettiest blossoms I'd ever seen, and every time the wind blew it snowed little pink petals all over me. I pretended I was the bride as I walked slowly up one aisle made by a row of trees and down another. Grandma found me there humming, "Here comes the bride, all dressed in white." We smiled at each other and I knew she understood. She'd been there herself once.

Dr. Glasser, whatever happened to the kind of love that makes dreams like that come true?

Your friend,

Ann

I was moved by what Ann wrote to me. Even though it was late in the evening when I read it, I decided to answer right away.

Dear Ann,

That poignant question at the end of your letter brought a few tears to my eyes. And you're not talking about the dark ages, you were nine years old, that wedding was less than twenty years ago. Truthfully, I haven't a good answer to your question, things couldn't have changed that much in twenty years. Maybe it has to do with the difference between small town values and big city values. All I know is that in a world where so many marriages fail, many couples your age are reluctant to risk that much commitment.

But what I point out in *Choice Theory* goes far beyond destroying marriages and even relationships such as yours and Mark's. All relationships are vulnerable to the deadly habits that are the natural result of the external control society I believe we all live in. That criticizing, blaming, punishing psychology is a plague on all humanity. As long as we use it, no relationship is safe from destruction.

While we will discuss this in person, I think you realize that your present task is to take good care of yourself right now. And if you find a new relationship, use choice theory from the start. I'd like very much to keep talking to you about love as you move into the next phase of your life. Call me when you think it's time for us to get together again.

Your friend,

Dr. Glasser.

Twelve

About two months after I answered her letter, Ann called and wanted to see me. When she came in she had a kind of resigned look on her face. As if she was wrestling with a problem that she had to deal with but didn't like it. The only thing that came to my mind was to say,

"You seem to have gotten up on the wrong side of the bed today."

"You couldn't have put it more aptly. For the past six weeks I've been on the wrong side of the bed. For me, there doesn't seem to be a right side."

"What are you talking about?"

"Sex. It's exactly what I told you would happen only worse. I thought it would only be a few guys but it seems to be with every guy I meet. Sex has become totally detached from feeling. Like it's an assignment that has to be completed or the night's wasted. It's become so separated, it's not even part of infatuation anymore. It's what the woman's supposed to do on a date even though the man is practically a stranger. It's a package deal. If the man spends any real money or makes any effort to show you a good time, you're supposed to go to bed. I mean I'm handling it but it's a drag."

"But you've only been dating a few weeks, how can you make such a broad statement. How many men have you met?"

"I've met a few. But I've talked to a lot of women my age. If the man's the right age, say between thirty and forty, and he's making a good living, sex is expected."

"Look, I'm a little out of the loop, describe one of your experiences so I can kind of get the picture."

"Okay, I met Tom in the supermarket. It seemed to be spontaneous but later he admitted he was out looking and I looked good to him. It was real smooth how he struck up a conversation and, I've got to admit he could talk. He's good looking, young, maybe thirty-five and we went up and down the aisles talking to each other. When we checked out he asked me if I'd like to sit with him in his car in the parking lot so we could get further acquainted. The lot was well lit, a security guard was standing right there. I was happy to talk with him. I was looking, too. Why not?"

"Did something happen in the car."

"No, nothing happened in the car, nothing's happened yet, let me finish. As soon as I saw the car, it occurred to me that sitting there with him wasn't as casual as I'd thought. That car was a knockout, a cherry red Jag convertible, it looked brand new. That Jag was made to impress. And I couldn't help but be impressed. We went through the usual getting acquainted routine but more and more the conversation centered on what a big deal he was. But there was also a little chemistry between us. Anyway, this was Tuesday but it didn't take him very long to ask me if I was free Saturday night. In a kind of confidential voice he told me he had an in with the maitre d' in what I knew was a very expensive restaurant. Mark and I'd talked about going there but we'd never had the nerve to go. Tom guaranteed we'd have the dinner of our lives."

"There doesn't seem to be anything untoward so far. Did he try to get close to you in the car?"

No, nothing like that, he was smooth, not crude. But still, as all this bait was being dangled in front of my nose, I began to wonder, why? Dr. Glasser, this rich, good looking guy who barely knows me is asking me out to a megabuck dinner. What's going on?"

"But you're good looking. He was attracted to you. I don't see anything wrong with that."

"I told him dinner was fine but dinner's not the whole evening. When you take a woman out to a place like that, say it's around eleven when we finish dinner, what happens next? We'll have talked for almost three hours. In a place like that, the wine routine alone takes ten minutes."

"The wine routine?"

"You know first he looks at the wine list, then he consults the guy in the uniform with the big key. Then he consults you and you don't know one wine from another so he makes the selection and the guy with the key compliments him on his discriminating taste. So right there in the car, I said, `Tom, I'm impressed. What happens after the great dinner? Do we just play the rest of the evening by ear or am I obligated to be grateful. He said, `No, there's no after dinner agenda. Girls who go out with me trust me to plan a great evening.' Well, you know what I was driving at. This guy picks up women in markets or a lot of other places and expects to get laid that first night, maybe spend the whole weekend at his place. You get the picture. It's exciting with every new girl. But when he saw I was less than bowled over he started to cool off perceptibly. I said, Tom, think very carefully, do you really want to take me out this Saturday and spend all that money. I'll be glad to go but I go home alone after dinner. And please, don't think because you just asked me out, you're obligated to follow through. I won't be at all hurt if something suddenly comes up and you have to cancel.'"

"Did he cancel?"

"No, not right away. He just sat there and didn't know what to say. To help him out a little, I said, `Let's leave our cars here. There's a Starbucks just across the parking lot. Let's go get a cup of coffee, my treat, and try to get to know each other. You have a good script, I'm just not buying a ticket to your show. But I am interested enough to want to have a real conversation with you.'"

"Did he go to Starbucks with you?"

"Of course he did. And he let me buy the coffee, too."

"When you really talked what did you talk about?"

"Our lives. He's lived with three women, one for as long as I lived with Mark. All three wanted to marry him but he's way too busy being in love with love to even consider that step. I told him about Mark and told him I was never going to live with another man again unless I was sure he was going marry me."

"Did you explain to him about being in love with love?"

"Sure. Why not? It's not that hard to understand. He got really interested. We talked for two more hours."

"How about the date, did it happen?"

"No, it didn't happen. But I did tell him if he was willing to spend some time getting acquainted I'd love to see him again to take a walk or go to a movie or have a bite in an inexpensive restaurant. But he wasn't coming to my house and I wasn't going to his for the time being. I did give him my phone number in case he wanted to talk."

"How long ago did this happen?"

"About a month ago."

"Have you heard from him?"

"We've gone to a movie, had a bite to eat and met once or twice in a coffeehouse. What he's become is a friend. I didn't think women and men could be friends but the way things are today men like Tom become your friends. I've only been out of circulation for three years but it's a different world out there from the one I left."

"A different world or a different Ann?"

"I guess both. I have a little better idea of what's going on."

"Do you like it?"

"Not really. It was fun getting to know Tom but with variations I've repeated that performance with about five guys in the past two months. A few of them even became slightly infatuated and that was a bit more interesting. But as far as I could see, none of them have ever been in love with a woman. In love with love and using women to get that feeling, is what they're all about."

"But women must go to bed with these guys all the time or they wouldn't keep doing what they're doing."

"Sure, they tell me about them. They don't use the word needy but that's who they look for. Tom even told me what he looked for in my cart, food for one like individual packages, that told him the story. What they can't figure out is why I'm not needy. It's not that they treat their women badly, they don't. I don't think they get to infatuation with most of them; there's not even that much feeling. Mostly, they go from going to bed to being friends, with very little in between. Love has nothing to do with the whole deal. I've talked to some of the women who've been through this routine. They're not that upset about it. They realize the guys aren't in love with them but they enjoy the dinners and the sex. I skip the sex and we go right to being friends. I'm not bored and I'm out and about. I'll find my guy, he's out there somewhere.

"But I can't believe there's so little love."

"Look these guys are an extremely common group, very friendly, a lot of fun but petrified of having a real feeling for the women they meet. But like you said, there are quality guys somewhere, I'll find one. But I don't think he'll be driving a jag like Tom. I do like that Jag, though. It was fun one weekend. We put the top down and took a ride along the ocean. At this point, Tom's much more interested in me than I am in him. If anyone's needy, it's him, not me. I don't want sex with these guys. But I do like the attention and I'm getting plenty of it."

"It's because you're playing hard to get."

"No, that wouldn't work at all, they'd see through it, they're not stupid. With these guys, I'm playing impossible to get. That's what gets their attention. I may be playing a game with them but it's my game, not their game. And the difference is, I tell them I'm playing it."

"You're adjusting very well to being back in circulation."

"Pretty well but not as well as I sound. I'd like to keep coming for a while if it's okay with you. How about if I just call you?"

Thirteen

I didn't hear from Ann again for another three months. This time she looked radiant, it was clear that things had taken a decided turn for the better. I didn't comment, I just smiled and waited. After, a few pleasantries, she started right in.

"Dr. Glasser, I may not know what love is yet but I'm more and more sure of what it isn't."

"Refresh my memory, tell me what it isn't."

"Okay, three things: it's never controlling, it's not infatuation and it's not being in love with love. I keep those three things in mind and lately I've had a little luck. Can you believe it? I've actually met two guys. I mean two regular human beings, unlike Tom, you know, men with feelings."

I just looked at her with interest and expected to hear about the new men but she changed the subject. I guess she was saving the best for last. Or had some other things she wanted to get off her mind first.

"After I read your book I started to teach my classes differently. I carefully read the part on education again and got further into applying choice theory to my students. More and more kids are getting the math and only two totally spaced out ones are failing. I actually look forward to school every day. Just getting that nightmare off my back, gives me a whole new outlook on life."

"Sounds great to me. I spend half my life struggling to persuade teachers to do what you're doing. But I'm curious about the new guys you've met. Anything happening that you'd like to share with me."

"Quite a bit, that's what I want to talk about.

"So, I guess it's over with Mark?"

"It's definitely over. I'm moving on. First I want to tell you about Ben. I've been seeing him a lot. I met him that Thursday, the same day we talked about Tom."

I noticed she was smiling as she continued.

"Ben owns a small jewelry store near where I live. Look. (She showed me a pretty pearl necklace.)

"How old is Ben?"

She must have sensed some skepticism in my voice because she asked,

"What makes you assume he's old?"

"I don't know, maybe because he owns a jewelry store. I'm sorry. Am I being presumptuous?"

"Okay, you're right. I don't know how old he is but he has a grandson. The little guy's pictures are all over the bench where he works. He's a good-looking man but I'd say at least fifty-five, nowhere near sixty. But you know what Paul Newman looks like now, I'll tell you he looks enough like him to be his son."

I was kind of surprised and she seemed delighted to see my reaction. She kept smiling and said,

"Love isn't predictable, is it? I never thought I'd get involved with an older man. I bet you didn't think so either."

"I'm sorry Ann; I just don't see where Ben fits in."

"Why not?"

She was having fun with me. I didn't say anything so she said,

"Say it Dr. Glasser, it's me going with an older guy that bothers you, isn't it? Does love have to have an age limit? What about all those older guys pushing baby buggies around my neighborhood? They're not all grandfathers."

She seemed to have a new confidence and was enjoying my discomfort. I liked the confidence part, not the discomfort. Anyway, I just went back to being my psychiatric self and said my usual,

"Okay, tell me, what's going on?"

She laughed. She'd made her point. Sometimes students ask questions that teachers have trouble answering.

"I needed these pearls strung. I'd seen a new way to string them in a magazine. I'd never gone into that little store before but it's near where I live. The first thing I saw was he had a tiny Yorkie who let out a couple of low growls to show me he was on duty. Ben said, `Fritz, she's okay,' and gestured I should pet him. Anyway, Ben and Fritz were so delightful I stayed over an hour. We discussed a lot of ways he could string my pearls and he told me to come back and get them late the next afternoon. Friday, when I came to get them he'd done a beautiful job and he charged me next to nothing. He then asked if I liked jewelry. I'd never thought much about it. He began to show me a lot of pieces he'd made and explained why they were so valuable and why this stone looked better in that setting and which stones enhanced each other. It was fascinating and it seemed natural when he asked me to have dinner with him. It was Friday night. I didn't have another thing to do. So we left Fritz in the store window, he loves to guard the jewelry, and went to a nearby French restaurant. We sat in the Chez Mimi for three hours talking and sipping some glorious wine. He told me his whole life story. He's divorced, he has two sons my age. One's married. He's the father of the little boy in the pictures in his store. After dinner, we strolled back and picked up Fritz. Ben invited me to come to see where he lives. I'd walked to the store, I only live a block away. I didn't have to worry about my car so I went. By then, I was quite interested in Ben and it was obvious he was enamored with me. Do you think I shouldn't have gone with him, I barely knew him?"

She was teasing me again. Obviously nothing terrible'd happened. So I said,

"He doesn't sound like a serial rapist. They just don't carry small dogs around with them."

"Ben lives a mile away in a huge, condo overlooking the ocean. I'd never been in a place like that. He'd told me he was comfortable but it was obvious he was rich. As the evening progressed, he seemed to get younger and younger. Anyway we talked until three in the morning. He wanted me to stay, there's a guest suite with, he made a point of showing me, a lock on the door. He assured me I'd have complete privacy but I went home. In the short time we were together, he said, he'd told me more about himself than he'd ever told anyone. But mostly he wanted to hear about me, starting with why such a beautiful woman was free on a Friday night. Anyway I told him the whole story of Mark, our breakup, including you and our search for the meaning of love. I mean the whole thing, the infatuation, the in love with love part and, finally, that I was searching for the in love with each other part. He told me he'd gone through all those stages since he'd met me at his store on Thursday afternoon. Isn't that romantic? On the way home he asked me if I would be interested in him. He made his case by telling me his father was still alive and in excellent health, that at his age, the men in his family were still in the prime of their lives. Dr. Glasser, what do you think of Ben?"

"Ann, you told me when you came in today that there were two guys so I know Ben's got competition. But from what you've just said, I'm not going to count Ben out of the running."

"Well, I've spent the last three months with Ben and, with him, my life's taken a turn for the artistic. He's introduced me to the world of music and art. And some theater, too, if you call opera, theater. He's bought me some expensive clothes and given me this small ring. He wants to do so much more for me but I won't let him. I don't want to take too much. But it's not as if he can't afford it and he's not the kind of man who asks anything in return. You'd have to know him. Ben is one in a million and, I'll tell you he's easy to be infatuated with. And besides, you're my teacher but he's become my counselor. He's always in the store and I can drop by any time and talk. I don't need an appointment. I guess that sounded like a dig, I'm sorry, I didn't mean it that way. And please don't ask me if I'm sleeping with him. I'm struggling with that right now and I don't want to talk about it."

"Fair enough. Is there anything else you want to tell me about Ben before you go on and tell me about the other guy?"

"I do, it's about love. There's no doubt in my mind that I love Ben. We've been together almost all the time for the past three months. I've stayed at his place weekends and we've gone out a lot, even during the week. I don't mind being seen with him. I actually like it. I look around at the people at all the places we go and I'll tell you I see a lot of women my age, or even younger, with guys who are a lot older than Ben. Once I saw a man who looked like Ben, only older, with a woman my age or younger and I asked him if that guy was his father. He laughed and said, I wasn't so far off base. His father is dating a younger woman but she's around fifty, about the same age difference we have. But, I don't know......."

There was a pause. She wanted to say something but she didn't know how to say it. I just waited. It wasn't uncomfortable, she was just getting her thoughts together.

"Dr. Glasser, when I'm with Ben I keep thinking about that part in your book you call, the quality world. Remember when I wrote you that letter about the wedding, that wedding was in my quality world. I want a wedding and all that goes with it. Well I want a husband and all that goes with that, too. I love Ben, but I don't picture him in my head as my husband. I hate saying this because I know he loves me. But he's too old. I don't want a man old enough to be my father. If I could freeze him at his age now and catch up to him later it'd be okay but when I'm fifty he's going to be around eighty. He tells me he'll leave me well-fixed but I don't want to give up on finding a man my own age."

"Have you told that to Ben?"

"I have. I told him that last night. I don't want to lead him on. That's why I came in here today."

"What did he say?"

"Ben loves me, he really does. He said that as long as I haven't anyone else and I'll see him, he'll settle for what we have. His love gives me a lot of confidence that I'm okay. That ordeal with Mark shook me up more than I realized. Anyway this is how good a man Ben is. He said I should keep looking for a man my age. If I find a man that's good enough for me, he'll give me a ring to celebrate that I've found the man I've been looking for. And also to remember that we once loved each other. He says he'll always be my friend. And with Ben that means a lot. I told him he can be the father I never had and he said, he'll think about that. But this is it. I think I've found the man. He's my age and I think he's interested in me. I haven't told Ben yet, I wanted to tell you about him first."

What's his name?"

"Richard, everyone calls him Rick. He drives an antique VW Van with bike racks on top and he hasn't made the slightest effort to get me into bed. This is serious, I think I'm in love with him."

"I think you're infatuated with him. It's too soon for love."

"Okay, have it your way, I'm infatuated.... Right now I don't really care what it is, it's wonderful."

"Do you intend to keep seeing Ben?"

"Sure, I said I've found Rick. I'm not at all sure he's found me. There's nothing between us physically, we haven't really spent much time together but we have talked and I feel something's getting started."

"How did you meet him?"

"I met him because of my success teaching math. When anyone succeeds with that subject, the news gets around."

"I can see where that can happen."

"Anyway, another school in the district, a middle school, asked me to come and explain what I'm doing. So many kids are failing math, it's driving the teachers crazy. I expected only a couple of teachers but ten of them showed up. They were all interested and four asked if I'd come and work with them after school. The district hired me to do it. It's fun and I make a little extra money. But this is where Rick comes in. He's the vice-principal and has to deal with a lot of the kids who act up in math classes. That kind of behavior is a lot worse in middle school than it is in high school. The teachers keep sending them to him and he's at a loss for what to do. But here's the thing. Unlike any administrator I've ever heard of, he's been attending my sessions and he's very supportive. The teachers were dumbfounded to see him there the first time and that he's continuing to come has really impressed them. He told me that even before I came to his school, he'd been talking to a lot of the kids and he was beginning to see it's not all their fault. What goes on in so many of those classes is more than most kids can deal with. Anyway, he used to teach history but he's also good in math and right away he began to catch on to what I was trying to explain to the teachers."

"But what happened, how'd you get together?"

"That's what's so interesting. As soon as the first session was over and I got up to leave, he walked me to my car. On the way, he thanked me for coming to the school. I thanked him for attending my session and pitching in with discussion and support. The next week he was there again and after the session he asked me if I had time to talk with him in his office. He began by asking me how I'd come up with the ideas I was using. I hadn't talked about your book to the teachers. I was kind of like you were with me at first, I wanted them to get started before I got into any theory. But with Rick, I told him a little about choice theory and asked him if he'd like to borrow my book. I had it with me to show to the teachers if it came up. He was happy to get the book and we had a long talk about school but then he asked me about my life and I asked him about his life, you know how that happens. What I found is he was so easy to talk with. He told me he was divorced and the father of a four-year old boy, Michael, who mostly lived with him even though the arrangement was joint custody. He didn't say why he was divorced but he gave me the impression that he wasn't involved with anyone else right now. But while a lot of the talk was personal, he didn't seem as interested in me as a woman as I'd like. Perhaps I was contrasting him with Ben, I don't know. That's the best I can describe it. But I hoped he was interested because I was very interested in him. He's gorgeous. After our talk, he walked me to my car and thanked me again for coming. All the way home I went over that conversation in my mind. There was something unusual about it but I just couldn't figure out what. I was still puzzled when I went to sleep but toward morning I suddenly woke up. There it was, what was bugging me. He and I'd had a choice theory conversation."

"What do you mean?"

"We'd talked over an hour without complaining about anyone in our lives. And for a vice-principal, struggling with discipline, he didn't seem to be the control freak most of them are. He was so positive and caring about his job and the kids. As I thought over the way he was in class and with me more and more it occurred to me that this may be the way he is. After that, I really got interested, I didn't sleep the rest of the night. All the next week, I made an effort to listen to what people were saying in school and even out of school and I'll tell you, the world is full of complainers. Then I thought maybe this conversation with Rick was an aberration, that it'd never happen again. But it did. The next week, after he'd read the book, we talked but again, no complaints, no criticism, so positive. We talked and laughed like we'd known each other forever. This time I knew he was interested in me. We talked a long time about what we think people need the most and how important good relationships are. Before, I left, I took the book he'd given back to me and read him those three sentences on Page 21."

She opened the book and began to read,

"To achieve and maintain the relationships we need, we must stop choosing to coerce, force, compel, punish, reward, manipulate, boss, motivate, criticize, blame, complain, nag, badger. rank, rate and withdraw. We must replace these destructive behaviors with choosing to care, listen, support, negotiate, encourage, love, befriend, trust, accept, welcome and esteem. These words define the difference between external control psychology and choice theory."

Dr. Glasser, Rick is someone special. Those sentences have begun to define our relationship, you can see why I'm so intrigued with him. I don't know if it'll last but, from the way he is now, I can't think how anyone I could possibly meet could be any more compatible with me than he is."

"Are you seeing a lot of him?"

"Not as much as I'd like but more and more all the time. We've really only known each other for about a month and a half. I met him about six weeks after I met Ben. Mostly what little we do is outdoors. We go bike riding and hiking. We can't really play tennis, he's too good, but we hit the ball together and I'm getting better. He's even more into fitness than Mark was...... But he won't do anything during the day on the weekend without Michael and that doesn't often include me. And he has Michael almost every weekend. Even if it's his wife's turn to have him, she's asked Rick every weekend so far to take him and he does. He's got a seat on his bike for Michael and when we hit tennis balls, he includes him for a while, then he watches us hit. I mean he's the kind of father every kid should have."

"But nights, the boy must sleep? And some nights on the weekend he must stay with his mother."

"Oh we have evenings but not nearly as many as I'd like. I still see Ben so I'm busy and that helps me to not bug Rick for more time. I think he likes that. He's on the phone with kids' parents almost every night and he does something I've rarely seen administrators do. He makes house calls. He says when he does that he really breaks through. I went with him once when it was one of the math kids so I could talk to his teacher about it. When we're together our conversation's about school, not as personal as I'd like but it's okay. It's building."

"I mean movies, you go out to dinner, it's not all school, is it?"

"We do a little of all that, like I said not as much as I'd like but we do it."

"But how does he treat you, what's going on between you personally."

"He treats me like he does everyone. Warm, interested, he's funny, I feel as if I've known him all my life.... But I'm puzzled about something, I need to talk to you about it."

When she said that I felt that puzzled was not the right word. Something was wrong."

"Ann, what's wrong?"

"It's silly I guess but it bothers me. We're very attracted to each other, the few times we've been together we hug and kiss, he loves to give me foot rubs. It's heavenly to get your feet rubbed..... But so far no sex. He's never indicated that he wants to go past where we are and my intuition tells me I shouldn't come on to him."

"Do you think he may have some kind of problem with sex?"

"I don't know, I don't even know why such a warm friendly guy is divorced. That's why I'm asking you."

"How long has this been concerning you?"

"I have to tell you the truth. I've been concerned from the start. Men don't act like Rick. Even Ben came on stronger at first. I don't mean they go crazy over me, I do send out a message not to hurry me but, from my experience, guys are usually more turned on than he is. He doesn't seem to be any more interested after almost two months than he was in the beginning."

"Could it have anything to do with his divorce?"

"It might have, but I don't know anything about his divorce. He never talks about it."

"What does he talk about that's personal?"

"Well, he keeps telling me that Michael needs more than just him. He needs a family, a woman in the house. His mother isn't that interested in him. Don't think I'm crazy but I get the feeling he'd marry me tomorrow if I were willing."

"Have you asked him why no sex?"

"I've thought about it but I just can't do it. I mean what would I say? Have we gotten to the point where it's abnormal for a man to go slow with sex? It's only been a couple of months, what's wrong with me? Why am I so impatient?"

"Is it your impatience that led you to say he'd marry you tomorrow. Where did that come from?"

"You're right, maybe it's all wishful thinking. He hasn't really said a word to me about going further. If he does, I could ask him about his divorce but right now I don't feel comfortable doing it. But please, don't get me wrong, he's a very sensitive man. He's so aware of the way I am it seems to me that he even tries to protect me from criticizing myself, the way I often tend to do. He's going slow, like there's no hurry. Besides I'm seeing Ben and I'm all mixed up. But I don't want to drop Ben. Maybe this thing with Rick isn't going anywhere. Maybe it's all in my head."

"Have you told Ben about him?"

"No, not a word. When I can't see Ben I tell him not to ask, why. He's smart enough to leave well enough alone. If this gets serious with Rick, I'll tell Ben the whole story."

"Have you told Rick anything about you and Mark?"

"Not much. I told him I lived with a guy for three years and we got along well. But then I decided I didn't want to marry him and we broke up."

"Didn't he ask you why you didn't want to marry Mark?"

"He did, he said, `You lived with a guy for three years and you didn't marry him, what was wrong?' I didn't want to get into all that stuff about being in love with love so all I said was marriage is very serious business. I cared for Mark but I just couldn't see living the rest of my life with him. That's a big step and I broke it off. I could see Rick was curious. He seemed to want to ask me more but he didn't. So that's where we are. We want to know more about each other but we're both afraid to pry."

"You still think there may be something wrong with him sexually. Is that bothering you more than you're willing to admit?"

"No, not really. He has erections when we hold each other, he doesn't make any effort to hide them. I just want more than he's giving me and I don't know how to get there. Tell me to be patient."

"So be patient. What's the hurry?"

"That's a good question. I want to hurry because I sense he wants to hurry. But not so much because he wants me, he's in a hurry for Michael. Several times lately he's said Michael needs a mother. He says he's on fairly good terms with his ex and while they have joint custody, she's really busy and he has him a lot more than she has. He thinks that if her family'd accept it, she'd give the custody over to him completely. Michael's getting close to me and instead of Rick feeling good about it, it seems to bother him. I don't really know what's going on. All I know is I care for him and I don't want to screw it up."

"How's Michael? Is he an okay little kid? There's nothing weird about him, is there?"

"He's a darling little boy. He and his Dad are very close. And Rick keeps telling me that anyone who can teach math to kids is the kind of person he likes to have around his son. I'm getting very attached to the little guy. That worries me, too. If I lose Rick I'm going to be doubly upset."

"Why should you lose Rick? Is there anything you haven't told me?"

"Nothing. I just can't figure out why he's going so slow and why he doesn't want me to spend more time with Michael and in the next breath tells me Michael needs a mother. I know I have to be careful. I don't know why his wife left him and he doesn't want to talk about it. Tell me the truth, Dr. Glasser, what's your take on Rick?"

"It may be you care for him so much you're reading things into your relationship that aren't there. Just keep doing what you're doing and go slow. And call me if you find anything out that I can help you with. I guess we can say that love has its mysterious side, too.

She nodded and we just sat silently for a while. Until she had more information, there wasn't anything else to discuss about him. After a few minutes, Ann asked,

"I wonder if you'd do me a favor.... Almost since the beginning I've been telling my sister about our meetings. For a long time she pooh-poohed what I was trying to explain to her. She was especially harsh when I broke up with Mark. She said, I was crazy not to put more pressure on him to marry me. But Edith thinks infatuation is love. She didn't have the slightest idea what I was talking about when I tried to explain to her about Mark's being in love with love.

She's never even gotten that far with a guy. All Edith knows is external control and as soon as she feels anything for a guy she starts trying to control him. But then, after I broke up with Mark, she changed a little. She started to ask me about what I was doing in school and about your book. I gave it to her but I don't know if she's read it. She hasn't talked to me about it and I haven't asked her. She did listen to the tapes we made a while back but, like I said, she pooh-poohed them at the time. She's also very smart, maybe smarter than me even though she never finished school. Even without a high school diploma she's moved up to where she's the head of the large office where she works. It was after they installed the computers that she really got ahead. She has quite a knack for computers. I think she could go much further if she had some education. But she won't try to get any because she still hates school, the external control turned her off totally."

"Edith may be one of those people who are supersensitive to external control. They have a terrible time in school."

"Anyway, I don't know what happened but now, all of a sudden, she wants to see you, not by herself but with me. The other day, she asked, `If Mark was allowed to come here with you, why not me?' Would it be okay if she came in for a time or two? She didn't tell me why but she said it had to do with what we've been talking about. What do you think?"

"It's fine with me, I'd like to meet your sister. But make it clear to her that this isn't therapy.

Fourteen

Edith was a striking young woman. If Ann could be described as pastel, calm and together, Edith was vivid both in looks and personality. No one could mistake her for composed and collected. Unlike Ann, who was soft, Edith projected an abrupt, not to be trifled with, image. Young as she was, she'd been hardened by a life of frustration and, as Ann had described her, deeply involved in external control. That was confirmed by her answer to the first thing I said to her,

"Edith, I'm very glad to meet you. Ann said you had a concern about our favorite topic. We've gone pretty far down that road, if we can help at all, we'd like to try."

"Well, first I've got to tell you I was pretty pissed about what you did with Ann. Before I understood where you were coming from, I blamed you for her breaking up with Mark. I thought he was the best thing that'd ever happened to her. She was crazy to throw him out.

Maybe I was wrong when I told her to put more pressure on him, to even get pregnant if she could. But I still don't think you know what you're doing. Guy's like Mark are hard to find. What's so damn good about marriage, anyway? I'd settle for a man like him in a minute, marriage or no marriage. My God, he even made an effort with my daughter. He's the only stable man Margo's ever known. She misses him a lot."

"But Edith's okay now. Last week, when I told her you would see us today she sat down and read your book. Edith doesn't have to read things twice, she really understood it. And then she actually listened to those tapes, again. She's finally accepted that I did the right thing with Mark. But she still won't tell me why she wanted to come here. Edith, you can trust Dr. Glasser, tell us why you wanted to come with me."

Then to our amazement Edith said,

"I think I'm in love. I mean really in love. I've connected. I've never felt like this before."

Ann said, "Who is it, Edith. Tell me. God, I think that's wonderful."

"It's not so wonderful. It's terrible. I don't know why it happened. But it has. I can't understand it."

I said, "That's what we're here for, to help you understand love and what's going on."

Then I saw a different side of Ann, the sister side, when she said quite abruptly,

"C'mon, Edith, we're wasting time, here. Who is he? What's his name?"

"His name is James...... I met him at a conference, out-of- town at a fancy hotel. You know how they send me to computer conferences so I can keep our office current. James heads the computer operations for a huge company. He's very successful. My job is nothing compared to his. The thing is I'm crazy about him and I think he's crazy about me. I don't know what to do."

We both looked at her like, what's the problem? But I didn't say anything. Then Ann said,

"He's married. You've always had a thing for married men."

"No, he's not married. He's never been married. And he's young. He's exactly my age. You know I've always been interested in older guys. Older Ann, not ancient, like Ben. But in computers, young is all there is. No one's old in this field."

Edith looked from Ann to me and back to Ann. She was like a cornered animal, with no place to run. We just kept looking at her. Finally she said,

"James is no different from any other nice eligible man I've known except .... he's black."

I said, "Edith, in all the talks Ann and I've had about love, we totally missed something you've just brought to mind. It's good, we can talk about it now."

Ann looked surprised, "What'd we miss?"

"Love doesn't perceive differences. You've heard the saying love is blind. Well, sometimes it is. It's certainly color blind, gender blind, money blind, beauty blind even power blind. Sometimes it's even species blind. Some pet owners love their pets more than people."

Ann pitched in with some dismay but with absolutely no prejudice,

"My God, Edith, you fell in love and had a baby with a druggie and a pusher. How can you think there could be anything wrong with falling in love with James? Calm, down. It's okay."

"I can't calm down. I've listened to all those tapes. All that crap about infatuation. I know you won't think we're in love, you're going to think that all we are is infatuated. Of course we were infatuated at first but now I think we're really in love and, if we are, we have some problems.

Ann said, "What problems?"

"His family, my family, I mean, what will Mom think? What'll I tell Margo? I could barely tell you."

I said, "Well, one thing you don't have to worry about right this minute is what anyone else will think? Edith did you really expect us to reject you because of the man you fell in love with?"

"Maybe not reject me but be a little more upset. Your being so calm seems phony to me."

Ann said, "Maybe you want us to be upset. Maybe you're the one who's upset and you want to blame us."

I said, "Edith, things like this happen. Before you start in with your families, you and James have to get together and make sure you agree on everything."

Ann tried to reassure her,

"I'm calm because I don't see anything to be upset about if you love each other. It's not like he's a bum or a nut. He sounds like a very respectable guy. Why don't you just stop wailing and tell us some more about you and James?"

"Yes, please tell us more. If you weren't really serious, I don't think you'd be this upset."

"But it's those tapes that got me so upset. You kept talking about infatuation, that it isn't love. I'm upset you may be right. I keep thinking he can't be in love with me. It's impossible. Maybe all he is, is infatuated. When he wakes up, he's going to realize I'm not what he really wants. I keep hearing people say that black men don't fall in love with white women, for them it's just a game. And I have to admit that when I started in it was a game for me, too. I never dreamt I was going to fall in love with him. But now I have. I'm sure I have. His race doesn't make a bit of difference to me. I'm ready to deal with that. But I'm not ready to deal with being played for a fool and then dropped. Oh my God, I'm all mixed up. I think I've fucked up the best thing that's ever happened to me."

I said, "But what did you do? Tell us what you did that makes you so sure you've messed everything up."

Ann asked, "How long have you known him, you never mentioned a word about him."

Edith kept wailing, "I didn't think it was going to last this long, I didn't want to tell you about a man I was just having a fling with. I know it sounds terrible but I didn't tell you in the beginning because I'd have to tell you about his being black. It was just a fling, why tell anyone? I've had a few flings with other men I've never told anyone about but this is different."

Ann said, "I'm glad you've spared me. But I agree with you, James is different."

I said, "Edith, please, calm down and answer Ann's question. How long has it been going on?

"Close to six months, we met about the time you broke up with Mark. And I really was infatuated in the beginning. I admit it. And when I get infatuated, I want sex. For me that's when sex is the best.

We were in bed in that hotel room ten hours after I met him. How could I have been so stupid? Why didn't I do like you're doing with Rick, take it slow, get to know him. How can a man respect a woman who did what I did?"

Ann said, "Edith, you're talking out of four sides of your mouth. You say he loves you, he doesn't love you, you should, you shouldn't, respect, no respect. Forget the tapes. Forget what you did. The point is it's six months and you're still seeing each other. Infatuation doesn't last. He would have long since dropped you if he were playing games with you. What I want to hear is what's going on between you now?"

I said, Edith, Ann's right. Tell us a little more about how you are together. What do you have in common?"

That question seemed to help Edith calm down.

"It's a little like Ann and Rick. They talk about school, we talk about computer programs. We meet at his office at night. He's teaching me to use some great new programs. And he's even teaching me to customize the programs we have. You can't go to any school and learn what I'm learning from him."

Ann said, "But he wouldn't be doing this if he didn't think you were worth teaching. There's a lot more going on with him than sex."

"That's it, that's what he says, I'm worth spending time with. As he teaches me stuff, he claims he's learning, too. Sometimes he stops and thinks for half an hour. You'd think I'd get bored but I don't. I try to figure out what he's thinking about and once in a while I'm right. It was when I started coming to his office at night that I began to fall in love with him."

I said, "Does he show any sign of tiring of you? Do you feel like you're crowding his life?"

"No, not at all. Everything seems fine, it's just that I know it's not going to last. I just know it."

I was baffled. But Ann seemed to understand why Edith was so discouraged. She said to both of us,

"I can see why she's so upset. I think you are in love with him, Edith. But do you realize what you've been doing? It was on the tapes."

"It's that damn external control. When I near dragged him off to bed that first night I made a mistake. I should never have taken control like that."

Ann said, "Edith, you're way past that night. It's not what you did then, I think it's what you're doing now. You just said it, that damn external control. What are you doing to James right now?"

I kept quiet. I didn't know what Ann was driving at. But Edith seemed to. She looked sheepish but she didn't say anything. Ann persisted,

"You did it with David. I think you've done it with every guy you've ever cared for. It's different because they're all different guys but it's really the same thing. What are you trying to do with James? Just tell us."

There was a long pause and then in a tiny voice Edith said.

"I'm trying to make him over."

"Okay, with David it made sense..... But why James? What's wrong with him?"

I just sat there. I still didn't know what Ann was driving at but she knew her sister. She had something very specific in mind and I think Edith had some idea what it was. Edith said,

"Did you expect me to accept David as a druggie?"

"I didn't expect you to do anything with David. I wish you'd never met him. But David's not around, James is. Now that you've fallen in love with him, like you just said, you're trying to make him over. But you can't. You know it, if you keep pushing, you're going to lose him."

"Okay, if you're so smart tell me what I'm doing."

"You really want me to? I might be wrong. You could get very upset."

"You're my sister, you know me. Go ahead, tell me. I think I need to hear it."

"You're trying to make James fit in. But, why? I just can't understand it."

Edith started to choke up,

"You're right. It's fear. I'm afraid."

"You love him, what are you afraid of? It doesn't make any sense."

"But it does, it makes a lot of sense.........."

She stopped talking, all we could do was wait. Then she started to explain,

"I love him, his race doesn't make any difference to me. But it does to him, It makes a lot of difference............ You see he's the only African American heading a department in that whole company. There's a lot of shit to take in that situation and he won't take it from anyone. I don't think he can keep being himself and keep his job."

Quick as a flash, Ann said, "Keep his job or keep you?"

Edith began to cry. She couldn't seem to stop. Between sobs she wailed,

"You're right, you're so right. I have been pushing him to fit in more. I'm more worried about him keeping his job than he is. More worried about what would happen to us if he screwed up his career, than I am about his self-respect. I am trying to control him. As soon as you said it, I realized what I was doing..... But how did you know?"

Ann said, "I knew because I'm struggling with the same thing with Rick. I want him to make love to me but he won't. And I'm having trouble accepting it. If I push too hard, I may lose him but I'm still tempted to push him. Accepting each other the way we are, that's the hard part of love."

Edith said, "You're right. If I don't lighten up and get on his side, I'm going to lose James. But I wasn't aware of what I was doing until you pointed it out. It's hard to let the people you love alone."

Edith began to cry harder.

I said, "Edith, now that you're aware of it, what do you think you should do about it?"

"Tell him. Tell him I love him as he is. He doesn't have to be anyone else for me. From the start he's accepted me the way I am and God knows I'm plenty screwed up. He keeps encouraging me to learn everything I can. He applauds my every little success. I've got to tell him how much I respect and appreciate him just the way he is."

Ann said, "I'd can't wait to meet him, he sounds like quite a guy."

When she said that Edith stopped crying. I said,

"I'm curious, Edith, do you know anything about his family. Will they accept you?"

"I don't know. It's never come up. But, if all of us accept him, it'll go a long way. I have the feeling from what he's told me, that his family all respect him, I don't think it'll be a problem if it's what he wants."

The sisters just sat there looking at each other. It was as if I weren't there. Then Edith started to cry, again. Ann hugged and comforted her but as she did, she started to cry, too. There was entirely too much joy in the room at that moment for them to handle. They left still crying. I walked out with them. Half way down the hall they grabbed each other around the waist and began to laugh. I could hear them shrieking with laughter as the elevator doors closed.

Fifteen

About three months after I met with Edith and Ann, Ann called and asked if I had time to see her. When she came in she looked relaxed and happy. If she was still worried about losing Rick she didn't show it. She began by saying,

"I wanted to see you because I want to fill you in on what's happening with me and Rick."

"I'm losing track of time. How long have you been seeing him, it seems to be quite a while."

"It's a little over six months since we met in that session with the math teachers in his school."

"Something's happened?"

"Very much so. Almost too much so. He's finally decided that whatever was holding him back is no longer there. All of a sudden he's dying to marry me. He's asking me with such conviction I can't believe it. Oh, don't get me wrong, I believe it. But I have to admit for a moment I was a little skeptical. But only for a moment, I'm not any more."

"You've made love and it works."

"No, we haven't. But he's asked me to marry him and that's what really counts."

"Are you going to move in together?"

"No, we don't plan to live together until we're married. There's none of the usual, `We have to see if it works,' argument from him."

"So you're not concerned anymore that he's still not ready for sex."

"Dr. Glasser, we're head over heels in love and then some. I'd sense it if there was anything wrong. He's sexual enough but he just doesn't want sex before marriage. Listen, last weekend, his ex had Michael and we spent two whole days together. Believe me, I was ready for it but he didn't make a move."

"What did you do all weekend if you didn't make love? Did you enjoy yourself?"

"That's a funny question, isn't it?"

"What's funny about it?"

"I mean the idea that a man and woman who care for each other have to make love to have a romantic weekend together. We had a great weekend. It was all outdoorsy, tennis, the beach, a bike ride. A cookout dinner in the park. A lot of talking about school and how things are better. Plus plenty of kissing and hugging. Besides he still gives me those wonderful foot rubs. Never underestimate reflexology...... Being with Rick is like a throwback to the way I hear things used to be, not the fifties, before that, like the movies in the late thirties. I don't think you'll believe this but it almost seemed like we were so in love sex wasn't necessary."

"I don't know what to say. You were there. You've been thinking about it. Do you think what you felt with Rick last weekend was love. You tell me. I guess my funny question shows how really focused on sex we've all become."

"I've been thinking about that. How we've made sex so important. As if there's something wrong with a man who wants to wait. Rick wants to marry me. If there were any problem with sex, he'd be avoiding marriage, wouldn't he?"

"It seems that way, but you never know. Maybe he's worried if he makes love to you and you don't like it, you'll reject him."

"That bugged me for a while but not anymore. Look, here's what I did. I decided to ask him if he'd tell me why he wasn't anxious to make love before we got married. And I came here because I couldn't wait to tell you how he answered that question. Anyway when I asked him if he'd talk about it he said, `Sure'. I was surprised; he didn't have any reluctance at all."

"I'd also want to know why he's divorced. Did you clear that up, too?"

"I did. It was very interesting. I'll try to remember exactly what he said. I started by telling him what a wonderful weekend it'd been for me. I asked him, if it'd been wonderful for him, too. He said. `Every minute of it. Don't you see why I want to marry you? We love each other, what are we waiting for?' I just up and told him what I was worried about. I said, `I'm worried because you're so different. That's not how people are nowadays. When they love each other, they start making love. I feel something's wrong. But maybe it's not you. Maybe the something is wrong with me. Tell me, didn't you feel something was missing this weekend? Please, level with me.' Then he said. `Sure, I felt something was missing. You went home Saturday night, we should have stayed together.' I told him, `I wanted to stay with you but you never asked, you never really made a move.' He said, `I don't plan to make a move until we're married, you ought to have figured that out by now.'"

"Then what did you say?"

"I didn't know exactly what to say so I just said, `But men don't do that anymore.' He said, `I'm not men. I'm Rick. I love you.' When he said that, I said, `Don't you think we should find out about sex before we get married? What if we're incompatible?' But he just smiled and said, `Ann, I love you. I'm not worried about us being incompatible, sex with us'll be great. My worry is you'll change your mind and not marry me. That maybe even now I've gone too far by insisting you marry me. But I just couldn't wait anymore. I want to set a date; we've known each other long enough. It's about time. We'll have plenty of sex when we get married.'

"But why, what led him to say that? I don't understand."

"You don't understand. How about me? I was dumbfounded. I didn't know what to say. All I could think of is if that's all he's worried about there's no problem. I said, `Let's set the date and the place and if it's in this universe I'll be there. I'm in no hurry for sex, I can wait until we're married. You've been this way from the start. I guess it's the way you are.' But then he said, `It's not the way I am. It's the way I am with you.' I said, `Why with me? What's so special about me that you don't want to have sex before we're married? I don't understand. And besides if you're so serious about love and marriage, why are you divorced?' He said, he didn't want the divorce. She divorced him. But now that he's met me, he's glad she did. I asked him if he'd tell me why she divorced him. He said, `I wanted to stay married. But I didn't fight it. I don't want to be married to a woman who doesn't want to be married to me.' I really wanted his opinion so I asked, `Why do you think she wanted to divorce you?' I didn't expect what he told me. He said, `Ann, look at me. My wife used to call me a hunk. When I met her we were in bed the first night. I was infatuated with her. All I could think of is I want her.' I was curious and asked, `Was she as hot for you as you were for her?' He then went on to tell me that she was and that her Dad liked him because he was such a straight guy. Her Dad was afraid she'd get involved with someone he couldn't stomach, she'd brought home a couple of those guys. But she also had a lot of ambition. She wanted to go to law school. Her Dad was a big shot lawyer. He didn't think she'd make it in law school unless she was settled down with a straight guy like Rick. You know, no drugs or drinking, that kind of guy. She and Rick were in college together. When they graduated, and got married, he started to teach and she started law school. Her Dad put her through and helped with the rent. She's now on her way to the big time; last year she made close to half a million dollars. Then Rick said and these are his exact words, `And here I am, just what you see, very small time. All I ever want to be is a high school principal. I don't want to make big money, travel, drink or party. I've no interest in a big house or fancy cars. And as long as I'm working with kids I'm never bored. And now I have my own son, he's the light of my life. I guess the best way to put it is I'd be completely satisfied if you'd be willing to share my life.' He said his ex was just the opposite. Quickly dissatisfied with everything. His being so satisfied with being a teacher, drove her nuts. The kid drove her nuts. He told me they never should have gotten married, they had nothing in common except the sex. Then he said again with a lot of feeling, `I'm glad she divorced me.' But I was still curious. `With all that sex why no sex with me? I still don't understand it. Don't you sense I want it? Don't you want me?' He answered, `Of course, I sense you want it and, of course, I want you. But there's something I can't figure out and it has me worried. You lived with a man for three years. You told me he was a nice guy. I'm sure you had sex. But you never told me why you broke up. I can't believe it was because the sex was no good. Was it?' I told him the truth, it was very good. Then he asked, `So why didn't you marry him? When I fell in love with you, which I think I did almost the day I met you, all I could think about is, if she was with a nice guy for three years and they had good sex, what was wrong? You asked me why I got divorced. I kept asking myself, why didn't she get married? You even seemed a little cool on marriage, you didn't want to talk about it. Ann, this is what I can't figure out. Why didn't you marry him? It doesn't make sense to me. I'm not about to start in with you sexually and have you leave me because I'm not good enough for you. It'd hurt too much. Besides it's not just me, I could stand being hurt but I can't bear the idea of putting Michael through another separation. That's why I don't want to play at marriage. If you love me, you'll marry me and I'll do everything I can to make you happy. What was that guy like that you wouldn't marry him? What in the world was so wrong with him?'"

"Rick was under the impression you rejected Mark?"

"Exactly. And you can imagine how I felt. I hated to have to tell him that it was Mark who rejected me."

"Did you tell him?

"Of course I did. I told him the truth. I had to. I explained that Mark kept telling me he loved me but he wouldn't marry me. His idea of love had nothing to do with marriage. I told Rick I would've married Mark in a minute if he'd asked me anytime we were together but when he didn't after three years I broke it off. Of course I was cool on marriage. I told him, `After what I went though with Mark, you implying that you wanted to marry me before we hardly knew each other, scared me half to death. I know you'll find this hard to believe but I was worried there was something wrong with you and you wanted me to marry you before I found out. You think you were scared, I was scared, too."

I said, "But now everything's okay?"

"Dr. Glasser, when I said that to Rick it hit both of us. He loved me so much that it was beyond his ability to conceive that any man could live with me yet not want to marry me. All he could figure is I must have rejected Mark and he was terrified I'd reject him. And I couldn't conceive that a hunk like Rick could possibly love me so much that he didn't want make a move on me before he asked me to marry him. Well, when we both realized this's what'd happened, we fell into each others arms. We were so happy we had tears in our eyes. I keep thinking of that O'Henry story, *The Gift of the Magi.* We loved each other so much we almost messed up the gift of our lives. Anyway, I told Rick about you and he wants to meet you. All this happened a few days ago and I couldn't wait to tell you. What do you think?"

"Ann, I think you've found what you once told me you didn't think existed in a love relationship: honest communication and trust."

"If Rick and I have anything, we sure have that."

"Okay, I'm still not sure either of us can exactly define it but it looks like you've found what you came here to find out. What ever love is, you and Rick have it."

"We're going to get married in the park. Everyone's invited and we'd like you and your wife to come. I've never been your patient so I don't see where you'd have a problem."

"Of course, we'll be there....... But in the park, what about the wedding of your dreams?"

"I'm getting the man of my dreams and I'll still have the gown and the cake. I haven't asked them yet but I'm sure Margo'll be the bridesmaid and Edith, matron of honor. And little Michael will be the ring bearer. It'll be a beautiful ring, Ben'll make sure of that. And, it'll be very old fashioned in one respect. We've waited this long, we're going to wait until our wedding night to make love. How about that?"

I had nothing to say. She could see how happy I was for her. She then said,

"All of a sudden we have a real family. Rick, Michael and now, James. James has a huge family, it's going to take him and Edith months to work out their wedding plans. They have to find a time when everyone can come. But for now we all hang out together. Margo thinks it's really cool to have a vice-principal and a computer expert in the family and they're all crazy about little Michael."

Ann got married. They were a stunning couple. It was a big wedding under the trees on a beautiful day. There was a soft breeze and such a warm feeling in the air. Ann had come to me unsure of love. I don't know how much I had to do with it but she's sure she has it now. I haven't heard from her since the wedding but one of these days I know she'll call.

Sixteen

A little over a year after the wedding, Ann called and asked to see me. She sounded happy on the phone and when she came in I couldn't believe how beautiful she looked, It was hard to take my eyes off her. If what was going on in her life had anything to do with what was going on in her face, things must be going very well indeed. I couldn't help remarking about how good she looked. She told me she was ecstatically happy with Rick. She said,

"I look so good because I feel so good.... But if you'd taken a closer look you might have discovered a reason."

"You're pregnant."

She smiled one of her delightful smiles and said,

"Our baby girl is due in four months. With Michael, now, we'll have one of each, a whole little family. All we need to complete the progression of love is to become grandparents, someday."

"Would you mind if we didn't concern ourselves with that today? .... But tell me, what's up with the rest of the family?"

"They're all fine. Edith and James are happily married, Margo is doing well in school and, as I'm sure you can guess, my mother is beside herself to see everybody so happy."

"Okay, Ann, I know you. You're here to do more than tell me you're pregnant and everyone's happy. What's on your mind?"

"Closure.... to wrap up all we talked about last year. I think we made a lot of progress in understanding love. But what keeps bothering me is we really didn't answer the question we started out to answer. Everything we came up with is important, believe me we've used it, all of it, and God knows it's helped. But it's not an answer to what love is, it's a list of things to do or not to do. You know, getting rid of the habits, negotiating, all that stuff. But when I came to you, if you'd handed that list to me it wouldn't have meant a thing. It was all the weeks we worked together to develop the list that helped so much. Anyway, Rick and I've been talking. We think we've come up with a clear, useful answer to what is love that could open women's eyes when they're in a dead end relationship. And maybe help the men they're with, too."

"But does it replace the list? I've been using everything we talked about with my clients and in my lectures. Especially, your idea of being in love with love. That's opened up a lot of eyes. And also love's progression, that it has to keep going somewhere or it stagnates. It's hard to conceive there's a simple, clear definition of love."

"Well, we think there is, that's what I'm here to share with you. But it doesn't replace the list. It just speeds up the process so women won't waste years and years like I did going nowhere with a guy."

"Please, I'd very much like to hear what you've figured out."

"Okay, first you have to understand I love math. I kept thinking, is defining love that much different from proving a math theorem. Is love so irrational that it can't be verified by logic the way math can?"

"Are you saying that there's some kind of logic behind all the goings on called love?"

"We are. Maybe not as elegant as a math proof but a lot more clear and to the point than what we were able to come up with."

I just nodded for her to go ahead.

"Okay. I have to give you a little background, something I read that got us thinking. It was an article in the paper recently written by a Canadian movie critic who was discussing how love and marriage are so distorted in the movies. All that's ever depicted is the infatuation that begins marriage and the misery when it ends. What goes on in the middle years, especially, what couples do in a lasting relationship is never shown. The critic admitted that this part would be hard to portray in any kind of an interesting way but still she wondered if there weren't some things that go on in good marriages that could somehow be shown on the screen."

"I can see her difficulty. It's like asking a newspaper to put good news on the front page. A story about a politician with a happy marriage would put readers to sleep. Do you think anyone would want to see what's going on with you and Rick on the screen?"

"No, we're not thinking of making a movie. It was the critic's question, `What goes on in a happy marriage?' that got us thinking."

"Okay, that's something we didn't cover. What is responsible for your happiness besides all the things we talked about?"

She paused and I just looked at her. I couldn't imagine what they'd come up with.

"Dr. Glasser, Rick and I loved each other when we got married and we knew a lot of the reasons why. But it wasn't until after we were married that we discovered what, exactly, love was. It's the success of our marriage that really helped us figure out what we believe may be a very clear answer to my question."

"Which is?"

"We think *love is commitment*. It's a metaphor, it's not a simile, love is like commitment. It's that simple, really only one word, commitment. If Rick and I love each other we are, by the force of that definition, committed to each other. Commitment says it all. It's behind everything on that list. It's the diametric opposite of external control. But it's more. It's action. It goes beyond the mysterious feeling that so many people think is love. Commitment leads to the progression we talked about. Commitment is doing things that get you close and keep you close every day you're together. Commitment is behind every word I read to Rick from your book at the end of one of our meetings in his office when we first met. Words such as care, listen, support, trust and negotiate, they're all an integral part of a committed relationship.

"But commitment is nothing new. Love, marriage and commitment are often mentioned in the same breath. What's different about the way you use it and the way it's been used for centuries?"

"What's different is that we use it as a synonym for love. For example, when I came to see you I asked you,` What does Mark mean when he keeps saying, I love you.' I couldn't answer that question and neither could you. Do you remember that?"

I nodded and said, "I remember."

"Okay, suppose before I even thought about coming to see you, I believed that love and commitment meant exactly the same thing. Then when Mark told me, *I love you*, it had to mean *I commit myself to you.*"

"Wait a minute, it means the same to you, I can see that. But how about Mark? For you and Mark to have gotten married it would've had to mean the same to him. For that definition to work, everyone who said he was in love would have to accept it. Do you think a guy like Tom would ever accept that definition. You would and he wouldn't, you'd be at the same place you were when you came to see me."

"No, not at all. I'm not saying Mark would have to accept the definition, I'm saying I'd have to accept it. And I would."

"Excuse me for being a little slow but I don't understand."

"If I had known that when I came to see you, I'd have told Mark that to me, love and commitment are the same. Actually, it wouldn't have to be Mark, I'd tell it to any man who was seriously interested in me as soon as I got interested in him. If I'd done that it would have scared Mark right off but it wouldn't have bothered Rick at all. He would have loved it. He'd had his fill of a woman who didn't believe that love and commitment were the same.

I looked perplexed as Ann was explaining this to me, it seemed too simple. I didn't say anything so she continued,

"You look as if you're having a hard time understanding what I'm trying to explain. Look, here's what I would have said to Mark. `You say to me, *I love you*. Can I take that to mean, *I commit to you*.' Mark knows what commit means, every commitment phobe, even that guy Tom, knows what that word means. Tell me, what do you think he would have said?"

After she asked that question, I had to think for a moment. She wasn't really misusing the word. If commitment was love it could be substituted for it. All she was doing was extending its meaning. Love is a verb in the statement I love you. I commit to you is the same. The usage is correct. In fact, I've been changing nouns like *depression* into active verbs like *depressing* or choosing *to depress* for years. Ann had read, *Choice Theory*, she knew I couldn't argue with what she was suggesting. And I couldn't. I said,

"Knowing Mark, I guess he would have said. `I am committed to you but give me time.'"

"And I would have said, `Fair enough, tell me how much time.' Mark was in business, there are no commitments in business without some agreement on time. The first time he told me he loved me I would have said, please don't use that word with me unless you mean you commit to me. If he said he committed himself, I say that I means we get married in a year or you stop telling me you love me. That's all the longer I'd wait now that I know what love is."

"But you loved him. That's an intense feeling. You knew he was afraid to commit. Would you have had the strength to confront him? It's easy to talk now that you're married to Rick."

"But you see connecting love to commitment changes everything. It would have given me strength. Before then, I'd always hoped love meant commitment but hoping and believing are two very different things. If I'd known then what I know now, before we went to that hotel for our first intimate weekend, I'd have explained to Mark that love and commitment meant the same to me. Please don't say you love me if they don't mean the same to you. I'm not saying I wouldn't have gone but I would have told him not to tell me he loves me unless he means he commits to me. It would have changed everything. Oh, I might have listened to him saying he loves me for a month or two before I called him on it. But not for years like I did. I believe it's hard for a woman who has any self-esteem at all to stay in love for any length of time with a man who refuses to commit to marriage. I remember feeling like dirt begging Mark to marry me for all those years. Sure, I broke it off eventually but look how long it took me and how much we both suffered. I'm not being selfish. Mark suffered plenty, too, by refusing to connect love with commitment."

"But how are you going to get the whole world to accept that new definition? It's a big change."

"I don't have to get the whole world to do anything. I'm not responsible for the whole world. Where love's concerned I'm only responsible for myself. What you do is your business unless you tell me you love me, then it becomes my business. But I have a feeling a lot of women are going to begin using this definition once they hear about it. Just mention it in a few of your lectures and, you'll see. At least with this definition, women would have a choice. They can still go ahead and mess up their lives, no one can stop anybody from doing that. But any woman who starts to use this definition has a much better chance to meet a man who loves her than she has now. She won't spend years hoping love is connected to commitment. As soon as he starts to tell her he loves her, she'll come right out and tell him that, for her, love is commitment."

"Have you looked up commitment in the dictionary, is it a plausible synonym for love?"

"Sure. I have. In my computer thesaurus the words that work for me are *dedication, devotion, promise and faithfulness* and a few more that are almost as close to the meaning of love. But it's not important that it's a perfect fit. If I'd used it with Mark, he'd have known what I meant."

"But you said, you had to be married to find this out?"

"We felt committed before we got married so we didn't think that much about it. It was after our marriage turned out so well that we thought: we love each other and we're committed to each other, is there any difference? When we couldn't find any difference in the meaning of the two words, that's when the idea hit us. Except, we believe the word commitment is so much stronger than the word love and so much more tangible. To a woman who is where I was with Mark, knowing that love and commitment are the same thing would make all the difference in the world. Talk to some of your clients about it and I think you'll see what we mean."

"I already have. We talk a lot about commitment and a divorced client just asked me, `What about the people who think they love each other and get married even though they really aren't committed?'"

"That's a good point. I guess they're the couples who find out too late that love is commitment and wind up in marriages that don't last. They never really knew what love is in the first place. They got married anyway hoping the marriage would fix everything. If women used this definition there'd be a lot fewer divorces."

"And a lot fewer marriages."

"And a lot less misery. Less marriages but more lasting marriages would be no tragedy"

"But need marriage always be the goal? Can't there be a committed relationship without marriage?"

"I guess so if they both agree they don't need marriage to prove their love is commitment. But that takes a lot of trust..... But if at any time one wants to get married and the other doesn't, the trust will die a sudden death right along with the relationship. Rick and I both wanted to be married because marriage is tangible evidence of commitment. We're not claiming getting married is a fix-all for a bad relationship or a must-do for a good relationship."

"I guess what you're saying is when you understand love is commitment, you know what you have or don't have."

"Exactly. It's a metaphor. Love and commitment are an invisible magnetic force that brings us together and connects us."

"Okay, you say love and commitment brought you together and connected you. Does that connection help the way you relate to each other? Does it help your marriage?"

"I was hoping you'd ask that question because the way we've worked it out, it helps our marriage a lot. Ordinarily, people who are committed will often say, *I love you* to each other. And we do, too."

I couldn't help saying in a half-joking manner,

"But if love and commitment are the same thing, don't you also say *I commit to you,* along with saying, *I love you.* It sounds sort of awkward to me but, do you?"

"We tried that for a while, but you're right. It was awkward and it seemed silly. Look it's a good idea, we use it, but we're not fanatics about it"

"That's a relief. I'm glad you're maintaining your grip."

"Okay, okay, but, as it turns out we did learn something valuable from saying, *I commit to you.*"

"You did? What?"

"After we said *I commit to you* a few times, Rick asked me, `Why does that sound so awkward?' I said, `I don't know, it just does.'

Then Rick said, `How about if I say, *I commit to our marriage*, does that sound better?' I said, `It does. I don't know why but it sounds a lot better.' Rick said, `Could it sound better because our marriage is something we own together and share? I don't own you and you don't own me. We're separate individuals. But what we share is a marriage.'"

"That makes sense, but tell me what you actually do when you're committed to the marriage."

"It' simple. Getting married doesn't mean we become one person. We will always be two separate people who want different things. Or want each other to act a certain way or do certain things to fit our own ideas or desires. You don't stop wanting your own way just because you get married."

"You're right, I hear that all the time when I counsel couples."

"But if you're both committed to your marriage, you solve the problems of wanting your own way by accepting that it can never be my marriage or his marriage, it's always our marriage. But here's how it works. As soon as we decided to get married Rick talked about us having a baby so Michael would have a little brother or sister. That sounded good to me so as soon as we got married, I wanted to try to get pregnant. But he surprised me and said he thought it best to wait a year. But instead of arguing or sulking, we said, okay, let's compromise. But we don't negotiate on the premise of what I want or what he wants. We base everything on what we each can do that's good for our marriage. That's what being committed to our marriage means."

"Let me see if I'm perfectly clear on this. Are you saying that the marriage takes precedence over what either of you wants? Your commitment is to the entity of your marriage not to your individual desires."

"That's it exactly. When we take care of our marriage, we're taking care of ourselves. If I'd kept after him to let me get pregnant right away or he tried to make me wait, it could have hurt our marriage. And since we love each other, we never want that to happen. Any time, he or I take precedence over our marriage, it suffers."

"I guess since you said you're going to have the baby in four months, you waited a while."

"Yes, I gave a little and he gave a little but the point is we agreed on a time we were both okay with."

"And if it hadn't been negotiable like if he told you he never wanted another child?"

"Then one or the other of us would've given in. Like you said when we talked back then, if we really love each other, one of us gives in. But it can't always be one person's way and never the other's. That would hurt our love and we've never come close to letting that happen. Actually, since we really love each other, everything is negotiable or unimportant, that's what keeps telling us we're really committed."

"Okay, one final question. From what you've just explained, you don't think people can really love each other without commitment?"

"Right, we don't because commitment and love are one and the same."

"But I have a commitment to many of my clients. Are you saying I love them?"

"I think you do. Actually, I'm not one of your clients and we've been committed to each other...... And I love you. Most of the love in the world is like ours. Good friends are committed to each other which means they love each other... Don't you love me?"

"Of course I love you, we've become very good friends."

"Doesn't it feel good to say it?

I nodded in agreement and asked,

"But if what you say is true, men like Tom can never experience love like you have with Rick. How do you explain them?"

"It follows, perfectly. Until they commit, they'll never experience it. They settle for infatuation and being in love with love. Actually, many of them settle for sex, they don't even get to infatuation. We're not saying they can't move on to love. The test is simple: can they commit to a sexual relationship? You saw Mark struggle with that in front of your own eyes every time we both came to see you. As much as he wanted to keep me, it was only to stay in love with love, he just couldn't commit. As long as he can't, he'll remain in that huge army of uncommitted, loveless men and women who don't know why they can't find anymore than short term pleasure. They're afraid to face the fact that love is more than a feeling, it is commitment."

"Oh, I just thought of something. What do people who are not in love or, as you say not committed to each other, say when they feel close, if they can't say, I love you?"

"Look, we're not discarding the first amendment, here. They can say anything they want. They don't have any obligation to explain anything. It's up to the man or woman to whom they're saying it to protect themselves. Caveat Emptor, let the buyer beware. But we add, let the buyer also be informed."